the other side of nowhere

danniella westbrook

the other side of nowhere

HODDER &
STOUGHTON

Copyright © 2006 by Danniella Westbrook

First published in Great Britain in 2006 by Hodder & Stoughton
A division of Hodder Headline

The right of Danniella Westbrook to be identified as the Author
of the Work has been asserted by her in accordance with
the Copyright, Designs and Patents Act 1988.

A Hodder & Stoughton Book

3

A CIP catalogue record for this title is available from the British Library

Hardback ISBN 0 340 89886 0
Trade paperback ISBN 0 340 92231 1

Typeset in Sabon by Hewer Text UK Ltd, Edinburgh
Printed and bound in Great Britain by Mackays of Chatham Ltd, Chatham, Kent

Hodder Headline's policy is to use papers that are natural, renewable
and recyclable products and made from wood grown in sustainable
forests. The logging and manufacturing processes are expected to
conform to the environmental regulations of the country of origin.

Hodder & Stoughton Ltd
A division of Hodder Headline
338 Euston Road
London NW1 3BH

For my angels: Kevin, Kai and Jodie

ACKNOWLEDGEMENTS

....

A big thank you to Beechy Colclough, the person who believed there was a person inside me worth saving. Thank you for never closing the door on me.

PICTURE ACKNOWLEDGEMENTS

....

©BBC Photo Library: 4 bottom left, 9. ©BIG Pictures: 7 top left and right, 8 top left and right, 10 bottom, 11 top. ©Gary Castle: 12 middle left and right. Tony McGee/celebrity pictures.co.uk.: 6 bottom left. Mirrorpix: 2 bottom left, 3 top left and right. ©Rex Features: 4 top Sunday Publications, 4 right, 6 top right Nils Jorgensen, 7 bottom ITV, 10 top left, 10 right Mel Bouzad, 14 bottom Granada. © Jeany Savage: 14 top right. ©Jeany Savage/celebritypictures.co.uk: 13 bottom left and right.
All other photographs are from the author's collection.

CONTENTS

....

1

HOW LOW CAN YOU GO?

....

I don't know why,
I don't know what
Makes me do the things
I know I should stop.

Why don't I question the faults in my head?
Maybe I'm frightened of what might be said.
People I love are slipping away
As my addiction grows day by day.

I'm trying to fight it.
I know I can win.
I don't want to carry on
Living in sin.

Danniella Westbrook, 2000

I wrote those words to my son Kai in September 2000.
By that stage my addiction to cocaine was so bad that I

and many others around me truly believed that I was about to die. I wanted to give it up, I wanted to stop, but I just couldn't, and I thought that if something did happen to me then perhaps one day when he was older and read this, Kai might understand how I felt. I hoped that he might come to realise that whilst I couldn't stop taking drugs, deep down I desperately wanted to – if not for myself, then for him. I was, at 26 years old, the most famous drug addict in the country, struggling to look after my three-year-old son.

To say that I had reached the lowest point of my life would not be an exaggeration. Through my addiction I had lost everything – except for Kai – and I had no one to blame but myself. The money I had earned during my career as an actress had long since disappeared. The string of properties I had owned, the homes we had once lived in, had gone too, along with the fancy cars and the designer clothes. I had squandered on drugs everything I ever had. And, worse still, through my behaviour I had managed to alienate all those who had ever loved me.

My old friends, the ones I had made before I was famous, had given up on me; the ones I had made through my career also tried to distance themselves from me. Those who wanted to stand by me and help me get clean I had no time for. Unless they used, then I simply wasn't interested. My fiancé Kevin wanted nothing more to do with me. Things had got so bad in our relationship because of my addiction that he had to close the door. He loved me, he wanted to help me, but he just couldn't. I wouldn't let him. Every time he offered me an olive branch I threw it back in his face. At that time he was suffering from his own demons. He was a recovering alcoholic and he needed time without me. If I wasn't going to get clean, then he would. He had to, even if it meant never seeing me again. As for my family – what can I say?

For my brothers, it wasn't easy being related to someone so notorious – especially for my younger brother, who was trying to make a career for himself in the police force. And as far as my father was concerned – well, he had lost his little princess and that just broke his heart. There weren't any harsh conversations, no lectures or shouting matches, just a sadness in his eyes that said far more than words ever could. You see, he, of all people, had never wanted me to be famous. He hadn't even wanted me to act, he just wanted the best for me – a happy normal life, a loving relationship, a couple of kids – and that's what he had spent his whole life working for. He would have given anything to us when we were kids, but what pained him most was that there was nothing he could do for me now.

It was just as bad for Mum. She, after all, had done most to encourage me in my career, and had paid for my singing and dancing lessons, because she so wanted me to make something of my life. Now she – the one person in my family who had once been so proud of

being related to the famous Danniella Westbrook –
reverted to her maiden name. Don't get me wrong, she
still loved me, she still sent money every week for Kai's
maintenance, but it had got to the stage where she was
ashamed to share a name with her own daughter.

Homeless and broke, I took a room above a social
club in South London. It was a dingy, dirty room right
at the top of the building. It had no carpet, no curtains,
not even a blind. In one corner of the attic room was a
manky old sofa that smelt of damp and who knows
what else, in another a filthy-looking small double bed
which Kai and I slept in together. The bathroom and
the kitchen area were communal and basic. Our one
luxury was a small television, which we would sit and
watch most of the day. We didn't have much, but the
way I saw it was that we had each other. I had him, he
had me, it was us against the world. He was the only
thing that really mattered to me, the only person I
could love unconditionally.

Most of the money I had, thanks to the weekly
allowance Mum gave me to care for Kai and the odd
royalty cheque I would receive from my agent, I spent
on feeding my son and the electricity meter. The rest,
I'm ashamed to admit, went on my habit, and when
that ran out there were always people around who
were more than willing to supply me with what I
needed. They didn't care that I didn't have the money
there and then. They would wait because they knew
that they would get it off me somehow, someday. As

far as they were concerned I was Danniella West-brook, I was famous. Whatever happened there would be someone to bail me out, to pay them back. And so they continued to feed my addiction, and I was so hooked on drugs, so addicted to coke, that I allowed them to do so.

By then my addiction was so bad that I was using drugs every day. When I got up in the morning I'd start using and would continue to do so throughout the day. Sometimes I was so high that I wouldn't sleep for three nights in row. Often I didn't eat. But none of that mattered to me – so long as I had my coke, then I was fine. Or so I thought.

The reality of it was a very different story, of course. I was far from being fine. Physically I was a mess. Twelve years of continual drug abuse had taken its toll on me. I weighed less than seven stone, and because I wasn't eating or sleeping properly my skin was grey, my eyes were listless and I frequently suffered from fits, many of which, to my continued shame, my son witnessed. The colonna of my nose – the cartilage that separates one nostril from the other – had rotted away. If I held my head up you could see that all that was left of the colonna was a small nodule of cartilage and skin dividing the two nasal passages.

My mental state wasn't much better either. When I wasn't having psychotic episodes in which I'd turn on my loved ones, I suffered from huge surges of depression and waves of paranoia. In fact the coke had made me so paranoid that I often believed that I was being watched, and during these periods I would tape up the doors and windows of that room and not let anyone in. When my drugs were delivered to me they would have to be pushed under my door. Sometimes I'd go for days without leaving the confines of my room, and when I did manage to venture out I was terrified. And, of course, if I didn't go out then neither did Kai. He was a three-year-old child and a prisoner in a squalid room with a drug addict for a mother.

It was at this stage that I realised I could no longer function properly, especially not as the mother of a young child. It simply wasn't fair on him. And so, having reached the end of my tether, I picked up the phone and rang social services and begged them to take Kai into care – for his sake. It was the hardest thing that I have ever had to do in my life and even now is one of the most difficult things to admit to. I wasn't doing it because I didn't love him. I was doing it because I did.

There is a view in many circles that if you keep your kids away from cigarettes and alcohol and from certain groups of people then you can stop them from getting involved with drugs but I'm afraid that that's just myth and I, of all people, should know.

I was just fourteen years old when I took my first line of cocaine. I didn't get involved in the drug because I moved in the wrong circles. I didn't start taking drugs because I was from the wrong side of the tracks – I came from a loving and secure middle-class family. And my first exposure to drugs didn't come through my work as an actress – it was a full two years before I won the part of Sam Mitchell in *EastEnders*. I took my first line of cocaine simply because I fancied the boy who offered to it me. It was as straightforward as that. I was induced to do something that I knew was wrong by a silly teenage crush on a boy from my neighbourhood – but I was so keen on him I was prepared to throw reason to the wind. Up to that point in my life I had never had a drink, never even smoked a cigarette. But by the end of that evening, the night I tried my first line of cocaine, I had also drunk the best part of a bottle of vodka and bought my first packet of fags. All it took was one tiny step.

Of course, when I first started taking coke, I never imagined that I would become addicted to it – no one ever does. It never occurred to me that by using the drug from time to time I could become dependent on it and that it could end up costing me everything – my looks, my career, my relationships or even my life. I thought it was just a little bit of fun, something to do at the weekends with my friends.

It was the late Eighties and cocaine was no longer something that only the rich and famous did. When I look back at that time now, it seemed as though everywhere you went you could get it, and everyone you met was doing it. You'd work hard all week then play hard at weekends – that's what people were doing then. It was quite normal to go out on a Friday night, have a few drinks and take a couple of lines. It made you feel more energetic, gave you that little lift when you needed it. That's how I felt, anyway.

I remember when I first started taking cocaine how sophisticated it all seemed. Once I was standing in a kitchen at someone's house snorting a line off this beautiful granite worktop through a £50 note and thinking: 'This is always how I'll do it – off a granite surface, through a £50 note.' It felt so glamorous, so right. How ridiculous that seems to me now . . . knowing that just a few years later I was doing it off the back of an empty packet of Marlboro Lights, through a rolled-up Tube ticket.

For the first couple of years I took the drug recreationally, in other words when I was going out socially, when I was offered it. But after that it wasn't long before I was completely dependent on it. Although I didn't think I was addicted at that stage, I did realise that I couldn't really function socially without it. If I was going out to a club, to a party or even for a drink I'd always make sure that I had some on me, or that I could get it. Cocaine, you see, made me feel better. It made me feel more attractive and amusing – generally more fun. It made me hyper. I was able to talk to people. Without the drug I felt like nothing. I didn't believe in myself and I didn't believe that I could live without it. As far as I was concerned coke gave me the confidence that I needed, while in fact the great irony of it all is that what it was really doing was taking it away from me. As a young teenager I had always been extremely happy-go-lucky and confident, at times I would say precocious even. I didn't need much encouragement to have a good time and I certainly didn't need any chemical stimulant. But once I began to take cocaine on a regular basis I didn't believe I was capable of enjoying myself without it.

The odd thing about a drug like cocaine is that when you are taking it you feel as if you are invincible, that you could do anything, be anyone, but the harsh truth of the matter is that by taking it like I did you are anything but. You are on a long road to destruction. At the height of my addiction to cocaine I was no one. I may have thought that I was someone but I wasn't. The reality of it all was that I was a penniless, out of work, single mother, living in one room above a social club. A dysfunctional, selfish person who had let her addiction grow so bad that she was now having to put her child into care. I had not only destroyed my own life but those of many around me, and that is something that I will have to live with for the rest of my life.

When, through the fog of my addiction, I could no longer cope, and realised that I was about to lose Kai, I vowed to get clean; I was determined to change my life. I thought that if he was taken into care for a couple of days, maybe even for a week or two, then I might have the space to clean up my act. But, of course, what I didn't realise at the time was what a long journey I was going to have to make. It wouldn't be days, it wouldn't even be weeks, it would take me seven months, a lot of suffering and heartache and a near death experience to give me the wake-up call that I really needed.

2

JUST AN ORDINARY GIRL

....

When you make a mess of your life it is always tempting to look back to your past and try and find a reason for it all, or even some person who played a part in your downfall. You can sit there and ask yourself time and time again what or who it was that made me the person that I am today. Why did this happen to *me*? Why did my life go the way it did? Why did I become a drug addict? Was it my parents? Was it my childhood? Was it something that happened to me in my past? Through my many years of being addicted to drugs and my subsequent journey through recovery I have asked myself these questions many times. But always the answer is the same. The only person I have to blame for how my life turned out the way it did is myself.

There was nothing dysfunctional about my upbringing. I didn't have a deprived childhood. I didn't suffer from any trauma during those formative years. In fact my early childhood couldn't have been more idyllic. I was adored by my parents, who provided me with a secure and comfortable family life.

I was born in November 1973 in Walthamstow and grew up in the leafy and affluent town of Loughton, in Essex. It was a nice area. It wasn't posh as such, but if you lived in Loughton then you knew that you'd done well for yourself. 'The boy done good' is an expression that springs to mind about Loughton back then. People who lived there mostly had a bit of money. They owned large houses with big gardens, some even had swimming pools, and there was always a top-of-the-range family car parked in their driveway.

My father Andy was a carpet fitter. My mother Sue for many years ran a clothes boutique in Woodford Green. Although, because of their backgrounds, they both considered themselves to be working class, I would say, looking back, that by most people's standards we were pretty well off. We always lived in nice big detached houses with as many as five bedrooms. My parents drove good cars. My Dad drove an E-type Jag and Mum had a Golf convertible. For a time my younger brother Jay and I were privately educated, and we had foreign holidays at least two or three times a year, when we'd go and stay in a rented villa in Florida.

My parents were both born and raised in Walthamstow. Money had always been incredibly tight in both households, and so my parents were determined to make something of their own lives. They worked hard for everything we had, and this was something they instilled in me and my brother from a young age. 'Nothing comes from nothing' was their adage, and it is a lesson that I have taken through my own life and one that I am trying to teach my own children now. If you wanted something in life then you had to be prepared to work for it.

Though he ran a successful carpet fitting business my father, for example, would think nothing of taking on extra work to make ends meet when money became a bit tight. Before we were born he drove a cab and would take on extra shifts when he needed to. My mother was the same. Even when she was running the shop and looking after us she would always have another iron in the fire, another project she was working on. She has never been one to sit at home all day painting her nails. She always had to be doing something.

By the late Seventies my parents had started developing properties. They'd buy a wreck, do it up and sell it on for a profit. They put a great deal of energy into this and it paid off. Having started out with nothing my parents, through sheer hard work and dedication, had made something of themselves and a life together. It didn't matter if all this wore them out. They never complained. They wanted the very best for us and they made sure that we had it. We were never going to go without.

We were a close family and my parents offered my brother and me a lot of love and attention. My father had a son from a previous marriage, and although Justin didn't live with us he was very much an integral part of our family. For a time when I was very young we didn't see him because his mother and my father were on bad terms, but when we were teenagers Justin and I became close. I adored him, and he looked out for me, and even in my darkest moments I have always been able to turn to him.

As a little girl I was certainly the apple of my father's eye. As the only daughter in the family back then, I was his little princess. Blonde, blue-eyed, with a cheeky little grin and a quick wit, I could wrap my father round my little finger when I wanted to. I was his 'Winkle', his 'Princess'. If he'd had his way I would never have grown up, I would never have left home! I would have stayed his little girl for ever. When he came home from work he always had time for us. He would ask me about school, what I'd done that day, what I was up to. He was very involved in our upbringing and always concerned about our future. 'What do you want to be when you grow up, Winkle?' he'd ask, as I sat on his knee.

When I was very young there was only one thing that I wanted to be in life and it certainly wasn't an actress. Like many girls of that age I was completely pony mad and all I wanted to be then was a show jumper or a three-day eventer. It was my dream. The sport was huge then and it was shown on BBC1 at 7 p.m. on a Sunday evening, and each week I'd sit down to watch.

My hero was a man called Harvey Smith, the champion show jumper of his day. I idolised him and wanted to be like him. One afternoon when we were watching the show and I saw him go round the arena without making a single fault I turned to my father and said 'I'd like to that! That's something I could do!' He looked at me and smiled.

I desperately wanted a pony of my own, but that wasn't going to happen. Children of course never factor in the cost of the upkeep of a horse or pony when they beg their parents for one. But even if my parents had had the money it would never have happened like that. Nothing came to us that quickly. In our family you only got things if you deserved them. My parents didn't like to spoil us. They wanted us to know the value of things.

Having no pony of my own didn't stop me from riding. My best friend Ginnie and I used to spend hours at the local stables where she kept a horse. I'd spend most of my weekends there, and when we had clocked off school we'd be straight up there come rain or shine. In return for doing odd jobs such as mucking out the stables, looking after the tack, or polishing the bridles and the saddles, we would be allowed to ride. Sometimes we would take turns on Ginnie's, sometimes we would ride other people's to exercise them.

For me it was heaven, and my parents were more than happy to let me spend time there. As far as my father was concerned it was a healthy childhood hobby and if, when I had finished school, I wanted to work with horses – even if I didn't make it as a champion show jumper – then that was fine with him.

But, of course, my life didn't work out like that.

At the tender age of seven I got involved in the world of showbusiness. Back then it was a world that I had never given much thought to, being so horse mad, but it all changed one day when a friend of mine, a girl from my street, won a small part in a Boy George video. She told me all about the day she had spent at the studio, what they were made to do and about meeting Boy George himself. It sounded exciting, and I wanted to do it too.

I wasn't a spoilt child but I was always wilful. If I wanted something badly enough I would do anything I could do get it. Because Justin wasn't living with us at the time and because there is an eight-year age gap between my younger brother Jay and me, for a long time I was the only child in the house, so it was easy for me to get my way. I would try to charm my way round Dad, and to reason with my mother, until I got what I wanted.

When I knew about what my friend was doing I nagged my mother till I was blue in the face to let me have a go. At first she was reluctant, but when she saw how much I wanted it she eventually gave in. My father wasn't happy, as he didn't want any daughter of his going on the stage, but he didn't have much choice in the matter. Once Mum had agreed that was that.

It started really with modelling jobs. I wouldn't say that I was the most beautiful child in the world. Certainly on many of the castings I went to there were a lot more attractive children knocking around, but I guess that I had the look that people wanted at the time and I was lucky because, most important of all, I was photogenic.

I modelled for the supermarket Asda, took part in a Weetabix campaign, launched the fashion chain Next's children's wear and became the face of the high street store Tammy Girl. I did a TV commercial for Opel cars and appeared in a Coca-Cola ad. It wasn't long before the modelling work turned into proper acting jobs, even if they were small. I got to play a child thief in Melvyn Bragg's *London Programme* and won a part in the West End production of *Joseph and his Amazing Technicolour Dreamcoat*.

I can't lie, it was fun. I liked working. Not only did you get the chance to take a day off school, where I was very unhappy, but you got treated like a princess. I liked getting all dressed up, having my hair and make-up done and all the attention that I got. And my mother liked it too. I wouldn't go so far as to say that she was one of those pushy stage mothers, but I think, in retrospect, she wanted that glamorous world for me. She was – and still is – a very beautiful woman, and before she married and had a family she had wanted to be a model. She hadn't made it, but now through me she had the chance to be part of that world. She wanted me to do well and encouraged me more and more.

I still went to the stables every weekend and enjoyed riding and being with Ginnie but my dreams of making it as a three-day eventer had faded. All I wanted to be now was famous. I'd had a taste of stardom and I wanted it badly.

It was around this time that I started taking Saturday classes at the Sylvia Young Theatre School in Marylebone, London. A girl from our area had enrolled there and she really seemed to enjoy it. My father was against the idea but my mother thought it would be good for me. I liked dancing and acting and was showing promise, so what was the harm in it? Eventually a compromise was reached. So long as I kept up with my schoolwork during the week then I could go to Saturday classes at the theatre school.

My career had always been a bone of contention in our household. My father has always held very traditional, old-fashioned values. He didn't get the whole showbusiness scene, he didn't care for celebrity. He was just happy for me to go to school, spend time at the stables and, if I liked acting, singing and dancing, then I could take the odd class in it. He just wanted what was best for us, and as far as he was concerned (possibly very wisely in retrospect), that did not entail being famous. I remember he used to say to us time and time again: 'It's not all about money. It's not what you've got, it's who you are. It's about being honest and true to yourself.'

A few years later when he was old enough, Jay also began to get showbiz work. He did a few child modelling jobs with me, the odd commercial. My father was incredibly unhappy about this. It was one thing for his baby daughter to like to sing and dance and perform, but he didn't feel comfortable with Jay being in that world.

Dad thought that it was abnormal for children to go out to work. He wanted us to enjoy our childhood and do normal kiddie things. Mum and Dad would have huge fights about it. I think he thought Mum was trying to live vicariously through her children, especially me.

'Don't cash in on the kids,' he'd say.

'But it's what they want to do!' she'd retort.

Unfortunately for my mother, by the age of ten Jay came to the realisation that acting was not for him, and one evening he announced to my parents that he didn't want to do it any more. He was an academic child and he just wanted a normal upbringing, playing sports with his friends and concentrating on his schoolwork. My father was thrilled, but my mother was livid.

'He's made up his mind,' Dad said. 'That's the end of it!'

'But he's got an audition tomorrow!' Mum shrieked.

'Well, he's not going and that's that. You heard him – he wants to have a life.'

Sadly, I did not share my brother's or my father's level-headedness. By the age of ten I couldn't care less about school or homework. I didn't want a normal upbringing. I wanted to be an actress. I no longer wanted to be the next Harvey Smith, I wanted to be the new Jodie Foster or Drew Barrymore.

Once Mum realised it was no longer a question of dabbling but it really was my dream, it became hers as well. But she knew that it wasn't enough just to want it: if I was going to make it then I would have to work hard for it. And, if I'm honest, there were times when, as much as I liked working, it bored me. Some week-ends I didn't want to be in a studio, but at the stables with Ginnie. There would be mornings when I didn't want to get up early and go to a job, afternoons when I would have rather been at the movies with my friends than spending long hours waiting to be photographed. I got bored with having my hair pulled about and having make-up artists fussing over me. I'd sulk and complain to Mum and tell her that I wasn't going to do any of that, I didn't want to work that day. And she'd just say, 'Yes, you are!' And that was an end to it. To be fair to her, it wasn't just about the time and money she had invested in me: I had pestered her so much, I suppose, about getting into that world, that she wanted me to be professional about it. I had a chance and she didn't want me to waste it.

There was another downside of working in the industry, which was that I was badly bullied at school. Throughout the early stages of my career I attended the local state primary round the corner from our home. I was never very academic and from the beginning I wasn't very happy there. But things got worse for me once I started appearing in magazines and on television. There was one girl in particular who had it in for me. She was a bully and used to pick on me because of my work, and managed to turn all the girls in my class against me. She accused me of being full of myself and told the others that I thought that I was better than them because of what I did. Nothing could have been further from the truth. I never thought that I was better than anyone. At playtime only the boys in my class would bother to talk to me, which just made things worse with the girls. Things got so bad that my only real friend in the school was Ginnie, and she was in the year above me.

One day during playtime when I was about eleven the bully grabbed me. She pulled me aside, out of the teacher's sight, got hold of my hair, which hung down my back in two long plaits, and with a pair of scissors from her bag chopped one of them off. A long thick plait of golden hair lay at my feet. I was distraught. I couldn't believe someone could be that nasty to me. I didn't understand what I had done to deserve it. She just laughed. I felt my world had ended. When Ginnie found out she was furious. She singled the girl out one day after school and beat her up for me. I don't think she ever bullied anyone again.

My parents spoke to the headteacher about the incident and took the decision to remove me from the school. My father was happy to send me to a local private school, but my mother thought that I should enrol full time at Sylvia Young's. Dad, once again, wasn't happy. It wasn't just the idea of me being at theatre school that bothered him, it was also the fact that I would have to travel on the train every day from Loughton to central London on my own. My mother's argument was that I was happy there, and after what had just happened to me maybe it was good for me to be in an environment like that rather than risk the same thing happening again at a new school. Once again he gave in.

The Sylvia Young Theatre School was and still is situated in Rossmore Road in the heart of London's Marylebone. The school itself was housed in an 1880s church school building, which had been converted into classrooms, studios and rehearsal rooms. There were only 150 full-time pupils at the school, which meant that classes were small, and it prided itself in having a family atmosphere. From my first day there as a full-time student I loved it. I loved the teachers and the other pupils, and I loved what we were doing there. It was filled with like-minded girls and boys who all wanted the same things from life. No one bullied each other, no one teased anyone, there was no rivalry, we all got on and did our thing. You didn't have to feel embarrassed for having a dream, you didn't have to make an excuse for having ambition and you didn't get beaten up in the playground just because your face was on the television the night before (even if it was only for a split second). For the first time in my school life I had proper friends and I felt like I really belonged.

The school week was divided into two. From Monday to Wednesday we went to normal classes – English Literature and Language, Maths, Science, History and so forth. I still wasn't very academic but the teachers were very encouraging and I suddenly began to like school-work, especially my English classes. The rest of the week we studied the performing arts – Drama, Singing and Dance. All the teachers there performed on the London stage when they weren't at the school. My dance teacher, for example, was in *42nd Street*, and another was in *Me and My Girl*. The highlight of each term was the school trip to see one of the shows, when we'd all go off to the West End and cheer our teachers on. Throughout the year we would appear in plays and skits, perform in concerts and dance evenings, and at the end of each term everyone in the school would take part in a big show, which our parents would come and see.

Sylvia Young herself was a mentor to us. She was very involved with all the children there and had time for everyone. If you couldn't get home at night because you had missed the bus or train, then she'd let you stay at her house. It was her whole life. She encouraged all the students there, and if any of us got put up for an audition she would personally follow our progress, and whether we made it or not she would always tell us in person.

It was the beginning of the Eighties, a couple of years after Alan Parker's hit film *Fame* about the New York performing arts school had come out. I had been too young to see the movie at the time, but like many kids my age I was hooked on the spin-off television series. And life at Sylvia Young's wasn't much different from that, although a little less glamorous. From Monday to Wednesday we would be in our school uniform taking normal classes like other children across the country, but come Thursday there we would be in our leotards, leg warmers and jazz shoes going from class to class, singing and dancing in the corridors.

While I was there I continued to work professionally. I made commercials, had more small parts in West End shows and did the odd television role, including a brief stint in the children's soap *Grange Hill*. I did it for the love of working. I realised that the more I did, the more experience I was gaining, and I stopped complaining to my mother. I soon learnt that all the standing around, all the sessions in hair and make-up were just part of it all, and if I wasn't going to put up with that side of things then I'd be better off doing something else.

All this time I had been earning money but I was never aware of how much I was making. I had been too young for that, and in any case I was doing it for the thrill of it then, not because I wanted to be rich. My parents had opened a bank account for me and were investing what I had earned, which incidentally was not a vast amount of money anyway. The idea was that I could have the money when I finished school.

Life settled into a steady rhythm and I was happy for my first two years at Sylvia's, but all that was to change when I was thirteen years old and Mum was suddenly taken ill.

She had been taken to hospital and was being treated there. Because she was due to be in there for some time I was sent to live with my Auntie Jean until she got better. Auntie Jean was actually Mum's best friend, not my aunt at all, but I was so close to her that she might has well have been related to me. I didn't mind going to stay with her at all and I was happy to be out of Dad's hair. Over the past few weeks he had begun to look terribly stressed and worn out. I wasn't sure why. I knew Mum was ill but she wasn't about to die. They had told me that she was having a hysterectomy, and as far as I knew hysterectomies didn't kill you. I did think it was taking her rather a long time to recover, but I wasn't that concerned. I went to see her at the hospital a lot and she always seemed fine to me.

I suppose, now that I have children of my own, I understand why they didn't tell me the truth. I guess they didn't want to frighten me. Cancer is a big thing to get your head round when you're only thirteen and all I knew about the illness then was that people died from it. My parents didn't want to me to think that I could lose my Mum. They didn't think it was good for me and they knew it wasn't going to be good for her. The last thing she needed was to be worried about Jay and me fretting about her.

I found out that my mother had cervical cancer not from my father or Auntie Jean or even from my elder brother. I heard about it from a girl at school. Most people would imagine stage schools to be hotbeds of bitchiness and bullying, but Sylvia's wasn't like that at all. There was a warm and friendly atmosphere at the school, and on the whole everyone got on well together, but there was one girl in my class I didn't really see eye to eye with. I wouldn't say she was a bully, but there were moments when she could turn on people for no apparent reason, and so I tried my best to stay out of her range. Unfortunately for me, one afternoon she was standing right behind me during a singing lesson.

My music teacher had singled me out during the class and asked me to sing a verse of the song we were practising. To be fair I have never been much of a singer, but I was a little upset when this girl started to laugh.

'It wasn't that bad!' I snapped, when I had finished the verse. 'If you think you can do any better then take my place!'

She leaned over so that only I could hear what she was saying. 'Oh, I'm not laughing at your voice!' she sniggered.

'Well, what is it then?'

'I'm laughing at you, Danni, 'coz your Mum's got cancer!'

In that moment I didn't know whether I was going to cry or hit her. I took a deep breath, bit my lip so I wouldn't scream at her and stormed out of the class, slamming the door behind me, without any explanation to my teacher. The girl, it transpired later on, had discovered my mother was ill when she overheard her telling the school secretary. Mum had wanted the school to be aware of what was going on, so that they would keep an eye out for me and make sure I was OK while she was in hospital. I grabbed my blazer and bag from my locker and walked out of the school. Once the door shut behind me, tears streamed down my face. I couldn't believe that Mum was so ill, I couldn't believe that they had all lied to me.

I walked from Rossmore Road to Marylebone station and took the tube to Bethnal Green. From there I walked to the London Hospital where she was being treated, crying the whole way. When I got to the hospital I went straight to her room but she wasn't there. I asked a nurse where I could find her. She said I couldn't see her at that moment, but because I was so distressed she eventually led me to a treatment room where Mum was undergoing radiotherapy. I wasn't allowed into the room, obviously, and had to talk to her via a telephone through this glass window.

'Is it true?' I asked, still crying.

'Yes,' she said. 'But I'm going to be fine and so are you.'

There was a calmness in her voice that was so reassuring but at the same time terribly unnerving. Did I want her, at that moment, to be as upset as I was?

It must have been so difficult for my mother. She had her reasons for not wanting me to know she had cancer, and she certainly didn't want me to see her like that or find out in that way. And I was completely unprepared for it too. There had been no gentle chat about what was going on from a loved one. No discussion about what her prognosis was, what chance she had. As far as I was concerned, from the moment I heard that she had cancer she was going to die.

When I got home that night I screamed at my father: 'Why didn't you tell me? Why didn't you tell me?' I said it over and over again but got no answer. He didn't say anything, because he had nothing to say. Dad hadn't really dealt with it himself, so how was he supposed to help me?

A few weeks later my father told me that if I wanted

to stay at the Sylvia Young school he was going to have to use my earnings to pay for my fees. Up till then my mother had being paying the fees, and my father had been taking care of Jay, who by this stage had been sent to a private prep school. Dad could no longer afford to support us both and he couldn't take on any more work. Of course, I didn't mind at all. Until then money had meant nothing to me, but at the end of that conversation it meant the world. And from that moment on I vowed that whatever I did in life I would stand on my own two feet and make my own money. Acting was no longer a hobby for me, it was my career. And I think it was then, at the age of thirteen, that I decided that my childhood was well and truly over.

3

THE FIRST TIME

....

I may have thought that I was grown up, but of course I was anything but. Earning my own money and being able to support myself through school did not make me an adult. Taking the train to school and back every day or doing the odd day's work here and there was hardly life experience, and yet in my naïvety I thought by my early teens that I knew it all.

After about a year of treatment my mother had won her battle with cancer. Everything in our family life returned to normal and I moved back home from Auntie Jean's. I was still studying at Sylvia Young's and still getting lots of work. Dad seemed pleased that we were back together, and the future looked bright and full of promise for the Westbrook family.

As a teenager I was given quite a lot of freedom. Of course, I didn't really think so at the time. Show me a teenager who does! But now I am a parent myself I realise that whilst both my mother and father held quite old-fashioned values they were also very fair with us as kids. So long as we behaved, worked hard and showed them respect, then we were allowed to act our age.

The problem with me, however, is that I never wanted to be *my* age. I wasn't content with that. When I was ten I wanted to be twelve, when I hit fourteen I wanted to be sixteen, and at sixteen, well, that was that – as far as I was concerned I would be a grown-up. I wouldn't have to answer to anyone. My Nan, who I loved to bits and was close to, used to say to me, 'What's wrong with you, Danni? Why are you in such a rush to grow up? Enjoy your childhood while you can, because your adulthood lasts a long time. Why can't you just wait and let it happen?' But her words fell on deaf ears. Why wait? What was the point when you could have it here and now? I always wanted things before my time, and whilst in one way, you could argue, this was the making of me, in another, much more serious sense it was very much my un-doing.

All I wanted in my early teens was my independence. Whilst most girls my age would lie on their beds at night and dream of having their first kiss, a boyfriend, a new outfit or a stereo, I lay in bed and dreamt of having my own flat, my first car and a great job.

And so at fourteen there I was, little Danni West-brook, thinking I knew everything there was to know about life. I had a career, could earn money and had regular work. I assumed that I was pretty streetwise. I knew things that most girls my age didn't. I'd seen a whole world out there through my work that was different and exciting. It was an adult world filled with professionals, from casting agents to photographers, cameramen, make-up artists and directors. And that's where I knew I wanted to be.

The funny thing, though, is that looking back now I realise I was actually incredibly young for my age and very naïve. At fourteen I had never been kissed and I didn't have a boyfriend. I had never drunk alcohol or tried a cigarette. Sure, I travelled to London to go to school on the train, but the reality of it was that I was really pretty protected from the outside world and I was still very much a child. And my interests as a fourteen-year-old weren't really that different from my peers. I liked fashion and make-up and watching TV. I liked going to the cinema, riding at the stables and listening to music. I loved to dance – not just at school in lessons but also at parties with my girlfriends – and I liked to listen to music on my stereo cassette machine in my bedroom when I did my homework. I was into Pink Floyd and Phil Collins. The only thing that really separated me from my friends in Loughton at that time was my burning desire to be famous.

Even as a child I was fascinated by the whole notion of fame. When I was little and wanted to be a show jumper, I didn't just want to be any old show jumper, I wanted to be the best there was. I wanted to be as good and as famous as Harvey Smith. That's how my mind worked. It wasn't enough just to work with horses, I wanted to be at the top of the profession and everyone to know who I was. Likewise, when I started in the world of showbusiness at the age of seven I didn't just want to be a child model, appearing in magazines and having the odd bit part in television commercials – I wanted to be a child star. One of my favourite films when I was young was *Bugsy Malone*. I idolised Jodie Foster, who played the lead role in the film, and wanted to be like her. I watched every movie she was in and followed her career avidly. I would watch *Grange Hill* after school and think how lucky those kids were to be part of that show, and when I eventually did win my small part in the series years later I felt as though I had arrived.

It was all about wanting to be something out of the ordinary. I didn't want to end up working in a bank or a shop. That world held no allure for me. I didn't want to be like everyone else. I wanted to be different and to stand out in a crowd, and for me that meant being on television or starring in films. I wanted to walk down the street and for people to recognise me. I wanted to be a celebrity, and now that I was at Sylvia Young's I was beginning to believe that I would be.

I had a large group of friends at Sylvia's, but when

it came to socialising outside school hours I was still very much a Loughton girl. At that age my parents wouldn't have me travelling to and from London after dark unless I was on my way home from school, and so at weekends and during the holidays I hung out with a close group of local kids. Loughton was a small place, which meant that my parents knew most of my friends, and if they hadn't met them personally then they knew of them. There would be sleepovers at other girls' houses, swimming parties and barbecues in the summer. Sometimes we would hold discos, because we all loved dancing, and if someone's parents were away there would inevitably be some kind of get-together at their house. My parents didn't mind just so long as there was an adult there to make sure everything was OK. Of course, more often than not, there wasn't, but we would all lie and pretend there had been.

My parents were fine about all this. They didn't think there was any cause for concern. I was doing what every other teenage girl was doing in my neighbourhood. I would be given a time to come home by and enough money for the cab fare. By this stage Mum and Dad had taken in a girl called Claire to lodge with us. She was, at sixteen, two years older than me and we became good friends. My parents figured that so long as I was with Claire, who they deemed sensible and grown-up for her age, when I went out in the evening I would be fine. In any case, there was no real reason for them to worry, at least on the surface. Loughton was a safe place and drugs were just not part of our world, at that time, anyway.

Everything that I ever knew about drugs at that age I learnt off the television. They weren't something that people talked about back then. As kids all we knew was that they were bad for you and something that you shouldn't do. In my early teens the cast from *Grange Hill* launched the 'Just Say No' campaign on the back of a plotline which featured one of the characters using heroin, and the message – that you should always say no to drugs – was broadcast in the form of a slightly out-of-tune single sung by members of the cast. I suppose the intention was good but the message of the campaign was really more about peer pressure than anything to do with the actual drugs. It was about not feeling you had to do something just because your friends did, but to be honest that could have applied to anything from bullying to smoking, drinking or sniffing glue.

So my knowledge of drugs at that age was pretty poor. I knew you shouldn't do them, in the way that you shouldn't really smoke, if you wanted to take care of yourself. From the TV shows I had seen I thought that if you took too much heroin it could kill you, but I had no idea that dope, coke, acid, ecstasy, speed – glue even – were all potential killers as well.

Drugs for me then were what criminals or the underclass did. Pimps and prostitutes took drugs, as did gangsters and low-lifes. People did drugs in fancy night clubs, or in New York, or on council estates because there was nothing else to do. I never imagined that people did drugs in Loughton and certainly not at our local bar. I had no idea that 'normal' people took them too or how easy to get hold of they were.

At home we never really talked about drugs either. Both my parents had come into contact with drugs. This was in the Seventies, when a few people they knew took them. Dad had a couple of friends who smoked marijuana, and Mum had a job at the Valbonne, a fashionable night club in the West End, so she had seen people use cocaine. But neither of them did drugs, they just weren't the type. They barely even drank. Mum has never been a drinker, and when Dad sat down for dinner in the evening he would always have a cup of tea and still does to this day. In fact he drinks so much of the stuff my children call him Grandpa Teapot. The only time I ever recall my parents drinking, and by that I mean having one or two glasses of something, would be on a special occasion – at a party, in a restaurant or on Christmas Day. And I can safely say that I have never, in my entire life, seen either one of them drunk. Merry, perhaps, but not drunk.

It was the same with my friends. Whilst a lot of kids that age experiment with smoking marijuana, we didn't. We weren't into dope. Sometimes at a party, if there were no adults around, some people would have a drink. Boys would arrive at the party with a secret stash of beers, and the girls might indulge in a little something sweet and sticky from their parents' drinks cabinets, but that was it. It was never anything serious, it never got out of hand and I certainly had no part in it. My girlfriends and I used to get our buzz from dancing. That's all we wanted to do when we were out – drink coke or lemonade, and dance around for hours to really loud and very cheesy pop music. Alexander O'Neal was one of our favourites.

But everything changed in an instant the night I took my first line of cocaine. I was out for the evening with Claire at a pub in Essex. I am not sure whether my parents knew where I was going, but I guess they thought it was fine because I was with her. In any case we would be meeting up with Justin, who was then nineteen and working in the City, so they knew that I would be OK. I always looked a lot older than my years, so there was no problem getting in. We had been to local bars before and my age had never been an issue.

I didn't set out that night planning to take drugs. I don't think anyone does the first time they do them. As I got ready for the night out it never occurred to me that that's what I would end up doing. The whole idea of taking cocaine was completely alien to me. I was fourteen and just wanted to go out and have a fun time with my friends. I'd probably have a couple of soft drinks and if I was lucky maybe even a dance or two. Of course it didn't turn out that way.

At the pub that evening there was a boy I had seen before and fancied. He must have been about nineteen or twenty and he worked as a broker in the City. I think my brother knew him vaguely. He was tall and dark, with piercing green eyes, and I was completely infatuated with him. I may never have had a boyfriend before but at that moment I knew what it was like to *really* like someone. I was besotted. I was talking to my friends when he came over. We started to chat and he was very friendly.

'Let's go out to my car,' he said after about ten minutes.

I wasn't sure why he wanted to go to the car. Maybe he thinks it's too noisy in here, I thought. Maybe he wants to get to know me better or even kiss me. I decided not to think much about his motivation and followed him into the car park. He got into the car – I remember it well, it was a black two-door 325 BMW – and beckoned for me to join him. I got in and started to chat away, and while I was doing so he leant over and opened the glove compartment and took out a CD. I assumed that he was going to put it on, but he didn't. He turned on his car stereo and we listened to the radio. From his trouser pocket he pulled out his wallet, took out a credit card and then a small paper package. He put the CD on his knee, placed the paper wrap on it and carefully opened it up. It was filled with a fine white powder.

'Want one?' he said. It was more of a statement than a question.

I had seen cocaine before on television, in pro-grammes like *Miami Vice*, so I vaguely knew what the substance in the package was. I always assumed that it was a drug that rich and famous people took – not people from Essex, even if they did work in the City – but I liked this boy so much that I thought it best not to make a fuss. I didn't want to lose face with him. I was desperate for him to like me. What harm can it do? He's doing it and he looks fine to me, I thought.

'Yeah, I'll have one.'

He emptied a small amount of the powder on to the surface of the CD, took his credit card and spread the powder around the plastic surface before cutting it into two lines about three centimetres long and a millimetre thick.

I knew that people snorted cocaine but I wasn't sure exactly how they did it. Fortunately for me, he took his line first. He took a £20 note from the wallet and rolled it up, talking to me as he did so. I can't remember what he said as I was trying to pay attention to what he was doing. Bending over the CD, he raised his left hand to his face, pressed a finger against his left nostril and snorted the cocaine up his right one through the bank note. He inhaled deeply, and as he finished he put his head back and breathed in and then out, as if to get the full thrust of the hit. He handed me the CD and I did the same. I am not sure whether he could tell it was my first time, but if he did he didn't say anything.

As I snorted the cocaine my nostril tingled slightly. The next sensation I felt was this horribly bitter, nasty taste slide down the back of my throat. I can't say it was enjoyable, in fact it was strange and disgusting, but within minutes of taking the drug I began to feel its effects. I felt this incredible buzz as the drug took hold of me. It was frankly the most exhilarating experience I had ever had. I was suddenly bursting with energy and I liked the feeling. I liked it a lot.

'Let's go back in and get a drink,' he said.

After about twenty minutes I was flying. I felt alive, I felt confident and up for anything. We were standing at the bar, queuing for a drink.

'What will you have?' he asked.

'I'll have a vodka and orange,' I replied without hesitation. I couldn't really believe the words 'vodka' and 'orange' had come out of my mouth. I didn't like alcohol. I had never tried it, but just the smell of it had always put me off.

I'm not sure why I ordered that particular drink, it was probably just the first thing that came into my head. Maybe I thought it was sophisticated. I took my first sip. It wasn't that bad, in fact it was quite nice.

The orange juice disguised the taste of the vodka and within half an hour I was on to my second. He offered me a cigarette. I accepted it and smoked it. I didn't cough, I didn't choke and less than an hour later I bought my first packet of cigarettes – Benson and Hedges – from the pub's vending machine.

I spent the rest of the night chatting away to people, my friends, the guy, even strangers, and when the music came on I couldn't stop dancing. I felt wonderful. My heart was thumping, as adrenaline pumped through my body. Cocaine couldn't be bad for you if it made you feel this good, I thought. I didn't tell Claire what I had just done and I certainly didn't tell Justin. He would have freaked if he knew that his kid sister had taken cocaine and had been given it by someone he knew. I think they must just have thought I was having a good time. And boy was I!

By the end of that evening I had drunk probably two-thirds of a bottle of vodka. I didn't feel drunk because the cocaine had counteracted the effects of the alcohol. I had also smoked most of the packet of fags. I didn't feel out of it, I didn't lose it – I felt great. I took a cab home at closing time and went to bed. As soon as my head hit the pillow I went straight to sleep, and when I woke up in the morning I felt fine. Coke *couldn't* be bad for you, I thought, it must be an exaggeration. I had just had one of the best nights of my life. It had been exciting and fun, and I knew that I wanted to do it again.

Nothing happened between the boy and me after that. We didn't have a relationship, but that didn't matter because I had just begun a new and much more serious one – with the Class A drug cocaine. It was the start of a love affair that would span the next thirteen years of my life.

4

THE FAME GAME

....

After my first experience with cocaine I knew that I
wanted to take it again, but it was three months
before I actually did. I was still only fourteen and
although at that time more and more people were
beginning to use the drug, none of my age group did.
In fact the second time I took coke was only because I
went to a party in Loughton thrown by an older
crowd. When one of the boys at the party offered me a
line in the kitchen, I didn't hesitate in saying yes.
Well, why not? It hadn't done me any harm the first
time I took it. I hadn't lost the plot or been hospi-
talised. It hadn't even made me feel ill. On the
contrary, it had made me feel great.

Over the next year and a half this is how I would
take coke – at private parties, when it was there and
when I was offered it. I may have done it three or four
times over that period. I never bought my own – I
wouldn't have known where or how to get it and I

certainly couldn't have afforded it. A gram of coke cost as much as £60 and my pocket money didn't stretch to that! To take drugs you needed money – money that I didn't have – but by the end of those eighteen months that changed. Soon I would be earning enough money to buy all the cocaine I wanted.

A couple of months after my sixteenth birthday I was put up to audition for a part in the long-running BBC soap *EastEnders*. The producers were looking for a fresh-faced teenage girl to play the part of Sam Mitchell, the wayward younger sister of the notorious Mitchell bothers, Grant and Phil.

Lots of girls at Sylvia's had been put forward for the part, so I really didn't imagine that I was going to get it. The producers were looking for a girl of a certain age and description who looked liked she fitted in with the screen family, so it was a veritable lottery as to who won the role. At the first audition at the BBC studios in Shepherds Bush there were eighty girls from all over the country waiting their turn and I remember thinking, 'I haven't got a hope in hell!' But within days I was recalled.

This time round there were only about fifty of us there, we read our lines and were sent home. Days later I was back again, doing exactly the same thing. There were ten girls left but I still didn't think I had a chance. In any case, to tell you the truth, it wasn't the be-all and end-all for me. I was right in the middle of my GCSEs and was far more worried about failing them than the audition. If I didn't get the part, every-one would understand and say I did well for getting that far – but if I failed my exams I would have my father to answer to!

I managed to make it through to the fourth and final call-back, but the timing could not have been worse. They wanted to see me at their Elstree studios, where the soap is filmed, on the afternoon of my History GCSE. I remember sitting in the school hall that morning not knowing what to be more frightened about – my History paper or the fact that I had to travel from Marylebone to Elstree on my own. It was the first time I had done that journey, the first time I had been to an audition without a chaperone, and I was scared that I might get lost or be late. As soon the adjudicator told us that our time was up, I put down my pen and held up my hand. I was excused imme-diately and I ran down the corridor, out of the school to the train station. I was so nervous my hands wouldn't stop shaking, but I managed to make it to the studio in one piece.

At the studio reception I bumped into the actress Michelle Gayle. She had been in a couple of episodes of *Grange Hill* with me and was now a member of the *EastEnders* cast.

'I heard you were coming,' she said. She introduced me to the boy she was with who was not much older than me. He had a nice look about him and a warm cheeky grin.

'This is Sid Owen,' said Michelle. 'He'll be your on-screen boyfriend if you get the part!'

Sid, who played the hapless mechanic Ricky Butcher in the soap, looked me up and down. 'You're a bit of all right,' he said with a wink. 'You can be Sam!'

I thought to myself, you cheeky git! I didn't fancy Sid, but I liked him right from the start. He was funny and charming and knew how to put me at ease. Michelle and Sid, who were on a break from filming, wished me luck and went off together arm in arm and giggling to the staff canteen for a cup of coffee. Initially, I hadn't been desperate for the part, but now I couldn't help thinking to myself, I like it here, I really do. This looks like a fun place to work.

I was directed to the audition room, where the other hopefuls were waiting outside. Of the original eighty girls who had been up for the part there were now just four. We stood before a panel of the show's producers, directors and writers and read from the script. They were sitting at the table looking at two pictures of Grant and Phil and kept placing them next to ones of us, looking for a resemblance. We read from the script over and over until, after what seemed like an age, they finally let us go.

I got on the train home and took a long, deep breath. I tried not to think about it. I tried really hard not imagine myself winning the part and desperately tried to banish any thoughts of working there at Elstree alongside people like Michelle and Sid. It didn't work.

*   *   *

Sometime after seven that evening, I was in my bedroom finishing off a piece of GCSE coursework when the phone rang. Then Mum called up to my room.

'Danni, you've got a phone call!'

I went to my parents' bedroom where there was a telephone, expecting it to be one of my friends ringing to see how the audition went. It wasn't. The voice on the end of the phone was from the BBC Costumes Department.

'Do you have any denim hot pants?' the woman asked.

'Er, yes, yes I do,' I replied, thinking it was a strange question.

'Good. Bring them on set tomorrow. OK? They're biking over the script to you now.' And with that she hung up.

I was a little confused. Did they want me to do a screen test? Then the phone rang again, and this time I answered, assuming it might be the woman from costumes again. It wasn't, it was Sylvia.

'Danni, are you sitting down?' she said. 'You've got it! You start tomorrow morning at ten o'clock!' She explained that I was on a three-month contract with the soap and that I would shoot my first scene the very next day. I just couldn't believe it. I put the phone down and sat there on my parents' bed for a moment trying to compose myself. I got up and walked to the window and looked out on to this beautiful view of Epping Forest. All I could see for miles were trees. It was as though time had just stood still. I couldn't move, I couldn't speak – I could barely breathe, I was so shocked. Take in this moment, I thought, savour it, because this is the point when your life changes for ever. Nothing will ever be the same again. This is what you have been waiting all these years for; you've got what you wanted. From now on you're in charge of your future, from this moment you are independent. And then the shock I was feeling turned to excitement. I started to scream. Mum, Dad and Jay ran up the stairs.

My mother, of course, was over the moon. Everything she had ever dreamt of for me had finally come true. All that time and money she had invested in me had paid off. The times she had taken me to singing and dancing classes, the auditions she had driven me to, the shoots and commercials she had sat through – had been rewarded. Even the terrible fights she had with Dad over my career, my lessons and going to Sylvia's had been worth it. I wasn't just another young hopeful with a dream. I had made it.

Dad was initially really happy for me. He gave me a great big hug. 'Well done, Winkle, I am so proud of you!' But as Mum and I started to talk excitedly about it, doubts crept into his head and he began to worry. Over the next few weeks he grew increasingly concerned for me. He alone had the foresight to see the damaging effect that this could have on my life. He was worried about how I would cope. I was only sixteen – too young to vote, too young to drink – and yet there I was about to be propelled into this very adult world.

He didn't see me as I saw myself – an independent, grown-up teenager, capable of paying her own way in life. He saw me as his little blonde, bubbly daughter. He saw me as a child.

I had decided long before I got the part that after I had done my GCSEs I would leave school. Technically, if I am really honest about it, it wasn't solely my decision! I had been quite a handful in my last year at Sylvia Young's, always getting up to mischief, answering the teachers back and playing pranks on the staff and other pupils, and they had asked me, albeit very politely, if I wouldn't mind not returning to school the following year. That had been fine with me. Not being academic I didn't see the point of doing my A levels. I was never going to be a brain surgeon or a lawyer, and I doubt I would have made it to university. I had planned to use what was left of my earnings to put myself through drama school and had dreamt of winning a place at the Lee Strasbourg School in New York. But now that I had won the part of Sam I no longer had to worry about my immediate future. I would be in the soap for three months. After that I would see what happened. Maybe I would still go to New York, maybe I would remain in England and get another role.

I couldn't sleep a wink that night. My head was just buzzing. I had read the script – I only had a couple of lines – and tried to steady my nerves. I just couldn't believe that tomorrow morning I would be shooting my very first scene.

I was on set the next day bright and early wearing my denim hot pants, a pink cropped T-shirt and a pair of Nike trainers. It felt surreal standing there on a set I had seen so many times on television. But there it was in all its glory: Albert Square, with its market, its caff, its laundrette and its famous pub – the Queen Vic. I was instructed by the director to walk through the market towards the square. Sid's character Ricky was to walk past me with a big pile of washing in his arms. As he passed me I had to give him a slightly flirty backward glance and he was supposed to be so distracted by this that he walked into a lamp-post.

We did it in two takes.

My first few weeks on the soap were like a dream. Everybody was really warm and friendly to me. Because the hours were so long there – we'd work six days a week from 7.30 to 6.30 – it was important that we all got on, and we did. The cast and crew became very much my second family, and their roles within the soap mirrored our relationships off screen. Sid and I became very close. Though we were not and have never been boyfriend and girlfriend, we were as thick as thieves and inseparable right from the beginning. When we weren't shooting a scene together we'd hang out in our dressing-rooms or in the canteen. We'd lie on the grass in the summer months and play football together with the other young cast members like Michelle. Once Sid and I got so bored hanging around on set that we decided to take the milk float for a spin round Albert Square, but Sid drove it too fast and turned it over. Neither of us was hurt, and we couldn't stop laughing, but the producers didn't seem to share our amusement. We were seriously told off that day.

People like Letitia Dean, Adam Woodyat and Nick Berry were like older brothers and sisters to me. A lot of them had started in the business at my age, so they were always helpful, and if I was having a bad day or finding things hard they would be on hand to offer support. I got on instantly with Gillian Taylforth. She is one of the most down-to-earth people I know and I still count her as a friend to this day. I was close to the older members of the cast too, especially Wendy Richard and June Brown, who were always so friendly and warm. I learnt a lot from June, and not just about acting. She taught me always to be polite to people whether they were the crew or the people in make-up and costumes. They were just as important to the show as the directors and the cast members, she would say. And there was dear old Mike Read, who I adored. He was not only good company, always making us laugh with his jokes, but he had a big heart too.

My relationship with Ross Kemp and Steve McFadden, who played my on-screen brothers Grant and Phil

Mitchell, was the same. Although they played East End hardmen in the soap, in real life you couldn't meet two more sensitive or caring men in the world. Even so, the off-screen relationship I had with Steve and Ross completely mirrored our on-screen one. In the soap they were my older brothers, always looking out for me, making sure I didn't get into trouble, and off set they were exactly the same.

In those first few weeks at *EastEnders* I didn't know how drastically my life was about to change. But Steve and Ross did. In those days *EastEnders* was filmed six weeks before it was broadcast, so although I had got into the swing of things on set I still had no idea what it meant to be famous. And I didn't really comprehend just how big the show was either. At the beginning of the Nineties, when there were still only four terrestrial channels and no satellite TV, *EastEnders* was watched by an average of 17 million people. If there was an exciting story-line that figure could rise to as much as 22 million. There were no reality shows back then, no *Big Brother* or *Pop Idol* for people to follow, so interest in the lives of soap stars was huge. On the morning of the day when my first scene was due to be aired there was a knock at my dressing-room door. It was Steve and Ross.

'Can we have a word?' Steve said.

They came in and pulled up two chairs.

'You can tell us to go away if you want, but we just want you to know that we are here for you,' said

Ross. 'We're family – not just on screen, but off as well, so we want you to know that you can come to us about anything. If you are upset about your work, if you are having any problems on set, if you are finding it hard, or finding the press attention difficult to cope with.'

'Yeah, yeah,' I thought to myself. You see, I thought I knew it all. I thought: I'm a woman of the world. I've been on TV before. I've taken drugs. I know it. They may be older than me, but what do these guys know that I don't?

But Ross continued. 'Let me just tell you that after your first scene is aired tonight, from that moment onwards your life will change dramatically. When you are sitting on the train, when you start driving and get out to fill your car up at a petrol station, when you go to the shops, things will stop around you and people will start looking at you.' Steve, who was always the quiet, thoughtful one, nodded.

'When you go out, watch your drinks,' said Ross. 'Be careful who you are friends with, watch everything, don't take anything off anyone, try and keep your friends about you. Beware of people who lull you into a false sense of security. There will be people who want to befriend you just because of who you are, be very aware of that.'

I thanked them for caring but didn't take much notice. Looking back now, how I wish I had.

I had only meant to work at *EastEnders* for three

months, but half-way through my contract the producers extended it for another year. The character of
Sam had gelled well with the others, and they wanted
to include me in more story-lines. Indeed, it worked so
well that in the end during that first stint on the soap I
stayed for another three years.

Ross and Steve had been right. Within days of my
first appearance on *EastEnders* the interest in the
character and me as an actress was phenomenal.
The public couldn't get enough of the simmering
relationship between Ricky and Sam and the show
was inundated with calls from the press. Sylvia Young
acted as my agent, and so requests for interviews
would be personally handled by her. Within a fortnight *Hello!* magazine had rung and requested my first
interview. That was a big thing then. *Hello!* was the
only real celebrity magazine on the stands and it was
very up-market. They didn't usually touch soap stars;
they liked royalty, models and serious actresses. That
was their idea of a celebrity. I was really thrilled and
so, of course, agreed to do it. But it wasn't just the
tabloid press and showbiz publications that were
interested in me. The broadsheets approached me
too. The show back then liked to tackle the big issues
of the day within the story-lines, whether it was HIV,
gay issues, rape or racism. Sid and I were involved in a
plot-line about under-age sex, so the press swooped in
on that. When that story was aired I was even interviewed by the *Daily Telegraph*, a paper I would never

have dreamt, when I started out, that I would one day feature in.

And as the press became more interested in me, so did the man on the street. Within a couple of weeks, just as Steve and Ross predicted, it became difficult for me to go shopping with my Mum or to the movies with my friends. It would be 'Oi, Sam!' and 'Stop being mean to Ricky, Sam' and so on. *EastEnders* wasn't a big budget show. We didn't have cars to ferry us between home and the studio, so at this time I was taking the train to Elstree every morning. For the first six weeks when I started on the soap I could sit in peace on the train and read my paper or book. As far as any of the other commuters were concerned I was just another teenager making her way to college or work. But when my first episodes aired that changed. It started with sideways glances, double takes and people whispering to each other, 'Isn't she . . . ?'

Yes, I was. I was the girl on the telly, the face they had seen staring out at them on the cover of their daughter's teenage magazine, or being interviewed on some daytime TV chat show.

It was all very sudden and a strange experience, but if I am honest I loved it all. I loved being famous, I loved being recognised. I liked the fuss and I liked the attention. I liked people looking at me and talking about me. I liked standing out from the rest of the crowd. I liked the idea of people wanting to be like me. I liked the fact that here I was, doing something that I loved and not only getting paid for it, but getting recognition as well.

I wasn't a nobody any more. I was someone at last and it felt great. It was a buzz, it was a hit, and just as it had been when I tried cocaine for the first time, after my first taste of fame, I knew I liked it and I knew I wanted more. Fame, you could argue, was my first addiction.

5

TEENAGE CELEBRITY

....

I would never say that being famous caused me to become a drug addict. I had, after all, been taking drugs on and off for two years before I joined *East-Enders*. And even though this use was purely recreational, there are many therapists I have seen over the years who would argue that I was already showing signs of having addiction problems as far back as that. You see, I have an addictive personality, I know that now and I also realise that whichever way my life had gone I would have been addicted to something – whether it was cigarettes, painkillers, alcohol, cocaine or even shopping – because that's part of my make-up. I have come to realise that I have an inability to know where to draw the line, when to say no. That isn't an excuse, it is a fact about me. It is the way I am and always will be.

But whilst fame didn't make me an addict, there is certainly no question about the fact that it played a significant role in me becoming addicted to cocaine at such a young age. And one of the main reasons for this was money.

By the end of the Eighties cocaine was no longer the drug of just the rich and famous. People all over the country seemed to be taking it. From Chelsea to Chesterfield, Islington to Ilford, cocaine was everywhere. Students would be taking it in their union bars, clubbers to keep themselves going on a big night out, models on shoots to stave off the boredom and hunger. Lawyers were doing it after a hard day's work, City traders in the middle of it, and suburban housewives to give themselves that little boost at a Friday night dinner party when it all seemed too much after a boring week in with the kids. You could find it as easily on a private estate owned by some member of the aristocracy as you could on your local council one. By then cocaine knew no social boundaries. But it did have a price.

Cocaine has never been a cheap drug and it is an incredibly expensive habit to have. Up until I landed *EastEnders* I could never have dreamt of buying my own drugs. Although I had earned money before I started on the soap, my mother quite sensibly always kept control of it for me. I would always have just enough in my pocket to have a good night out with the girls. Enough to buy a couple of drinks, to pay my cab fares and maybe have some change for something to eat on the way home, but I didn't have enough for drugs.

Once I started working full time, though, that changed. My first pay packet on the soap wasn't vast by today's standards or as much as I earned later on in my career, but it was easily five times as much as my friends in full-time employment were pulling in. It was a staggering amount of money for a girl my age to be making. I changed instantly from a kid who could afford a night out with her friends, the odd bit of make-up or new outfit to one who could afford to buy a car or put down a deposit on a flat if I wanted to. And that's exactly what I did. Within a year of being on the soap I bought my first property – a three-bedroom flat in Woodford – and my first car – a convertible Vitara. And I still had money left in the bank.

It all seemed a bit surreal. I had always wanted to earn my keep, to stand on my own two feet, but it never dawned on me before I got the part that I would be paid that much money. Suddenly, I could afford to go on holiday and take my friends with me. I could buy designer clothes, eat in restaurants, and if I wanted to take cocaine, I no longer had to rely on other people to give me a line. I could now afford to buy my own.

It was, in fact, quite a while before I did buy my first gram. It wasn't a case of me being in the soap for a couple of weeks and straightaway blowing my first wage packet on an ounce of cocaine and becoming an addict overnight. It didn't happen like that. It rarely does. Maybe it was a couple of months, maybe it was longer. I can't honestly tell you. But what I do remember was just how terrifyingly easy it was.

The first time I bought a gram of coke I didn't have to go to some dodgy dealer. I didn't get if off a housing estate or in a dark alleyway. I got it from a guy I met at a private party in Essex. I heard on the grapevine that he was 'carrying'. He didn't look like a drug dealer. He didn't look like an addict. He looked like anyone else. The kind of guy you could introduce to your parents without having to worry. And so I approached him and asked whether I could buy some coke. And he said yes. It was that simple. I handed him the money, he handed me the wrap and that was that. Done deal.

When I first started on *EastEnders* I was still living at home with my parents and seeing my old friends. Life on that front remained quite normal for a while. I'd be on set all day working, hanging out with the cast and crew; and then, come the weekend, I would be with friends and family.

Now that I was older and 'of age' as far as Mum and Dad were concerned, I had a lot more freedom. I was no longer having sleepovers and disco parties with my girlfriends. We were going to bars and clubs in the area on a regular basis. The odd evening out with Claire had become routine.

A night out with the girls always started the same way. We'd all turn up at someone's house and get ready together. In many ways this was the highlight of the entire night. It was a chance for us to catch up and have a giggle. We would begin with putting on the stereo, cranking it up to full volume and then all cram in front of the mirror in the bedroom to do our hair and make-up. We'd fret over what to wear, have a gossip and exchange views about which boys we liked and which ones we didn't. It was our little ritual and we loved it.

Then we'd hop in a cab and head out. We would usually start at a local bar. There was a wine bar we liked to go to in Chingford called Toots, and another popular one was Charlie Chan's. Sometimes, if we were having a big evening out, we'd end up at The Country Club, in Epping. On very special occasions we'd head up West and do the club scene.

We didn't do drugs on a night out together. Though I had taken them and would do so whenever they were offered to me, my friends didn't. It wasn't their thing. If I did take them during that time I would do so out of sight. Maybe my friends knew then. Maybe they didn't. If they did they didn't say anything. It was never an issue.

My friends and I were nicknamed the 'vodka, lime and soda' girls, because that's all we ever drank. We never had to think about what to order when we went to a bar. It was always 'vodka, lime and soda'. So a good night for us was: get ready, go out, have a drink, have a laugh and a dance. Afterwards we'd stop off at the local kebab house or chippie and grab ourselves something to eat and then we'd be off home.

And so this is how it was for a while. What I would call, looking back, just good clean harmless, old-fashioned fun. Nothing bad, certainly nothing illegal, and nothing to worry about. We weren't binge drinking, we weren't causing or getting ourselves into trouble. We liked boys, yes, but we never got into compromising situations, we were all much too sensible for that. We simply behaved like most other teenage girls did around that time.

But, of course, the problem was that I wasn't like most girls. I was earning the kind of money at the beginning of my career that most adults would be happy to earn at the top of theirs. I can't tell you exactly how much I got paid because I wasn't in control of my money then. *EastEnders* would pay Sylvia Young, who acted as my agent, and she would transfer the money to my mother. Each monthly cheque would then be divided and paid into three separate bank accounts – a savings account, a tax account and a spending account. The only money I had access to was my spending account, and if I didn't have enough money in it to buy what I wanted then I would have to ask my parents for permission to take money from my savings.

Although I liked the feeling that I was earning 'proper' money, the cash itself didn't really interest me at first. During those initial months, before my contract was extended, it was all about the love of the job rather than the financial gain. I was living at home so I had no overheads, and I wasn't into restaurants or designer dresses or shoes. I was still shopping for clothes on the high street with my mother. In any case I didn't really have the time to spend the money. If I had a good plot-line then I would be working six days a week, and in those first few months I was so blown away by the fact that I had been given this great opportunity to prove myself as an actress that all I wanted to do was work hard and show people what I could do. But after a while the complacency set in. With my contract extended for another year I felt secure in what I was doing. The part became second nature to me and I no longer felt that I had to give my all. I liked working but I was also young and I wanted to have a good time.

It was around this time that I started to get invited to more and more 'celebrity' events. There were award ceremonies and premières, evenings at West End bars and parties at private members' clubs. It was a whole new scene. It was fun, exciting, exotic and far more glamorous than anything I had known back home. I was beginning to become well known, but nowhere near as famous as some of the people I was mixing with. So at first I was captivated by the whole novelty of just being in the same room as a famous model, actor, pop star or even – if I went to a film première – a member of the Royal family.

This was an older and more sophisticated crowd of people. They had style and money, they had lived a little, and even though I was still just a teenager I wanted to be part of that world. But if I was going to fit in with that set then I knew I would have to change.

For a time, I suppose, I lived a double life. During the week I would go to a couple of these parties with Sid or other members of the cast, and then at weekends I would go back to being a local Loughton girl. I'd see my friends and would always, without fail, sit down to one of my mother's roasts on a Sunday with my family. But as I became increasingly seduced by the party scene I began to tire of my old life. Hanging out with my girlfriends locally on a Saturday night was no longer such a big deal for me. Who wanted to spend the evening at Charlie Chan's or Toots when you could be hanging out at sophisticated, glamorous clubs like Browns, Legends or the Emporium? Don't get me wrong, I still loved my friends but I'd seen a whole new world out there and decided almost without thinking about it that I had moved on.

Most of my friends couldn't afford to go out in the middle of the week. Even if they could, many would have refused on the grounds that they had to be up early the next day for work or college, but for me it was different. I could always argue to myself that this *was* work. Turning up at an event, being seen, getting noticed – it was all part of the job. The more you were seen out, the higher your profile. The higher your profile, the more work you'd get in the future. It made perfect sense to me.

And I was right. Having played the game for a

couple of months it wasn't long before I started to get more extracurricular work outside the soap. I was invited to do modelling work for magazines and newspapers, and Sid and I would frequently do cover stories for the television press. The BBC didn't mind – I could do as many interviews and shoots as I liked so long as it promoted the show – and there was no shortage of offers. I could be paid anything from £1,000 to £4,000 for a job, and sometimes I would do as many as two a month. Within a short time I had almost trebled my annual earning capacity.

My new lifestyle gave me a taste for money. Suddenly it mattered to me and I began to want it. It wasn't the be-all and end-all for me: I still loved the job itself and, frankly, would have done it for free if I'd had to, but now I had money I found I liked it, and I realised that if I wanted to move in this new circle then I needed it.

My changing attitudes were worrying my parents, though, and money quickly became a contentious issue in the Westbrook household. My father had never stopped being concerned about whether I was old enough to cope with the fame and all that came with it. He was all too well aware of the fact that fame had its price and he would, in his own gentle way, often sit me down and talk to me about this. But, of course, I was blind to it. As far as I was concerned fame didn't cost you anything, fame only brought fortune. What was wrong with being famous if within the space of just a year you could afford what most people spend a lifetime saving for? His outlook didn't make sense to me. But Dad was always cautious like that. My parents had made money and were comfortably off, but that was through graft and prudence. It had been a slow and steady process, one that had taught them the significance of money.

Knowing all about the property market, my parents had encouraged me to invest in my first flat. It made complete sense to them and they were pleased that I had made it on to the property ladder. As far as my father was concerned, even if my career didn't last then at least I would have a roof over my head. When I bought the flat in Woodford it was a complete wreck, and it was a long time before I moved in, which they were both relieved about. And I was happy about that too. I loved the idea of owning my own place, and doing it up, making it all nice, but if I am honest about it, despite my burning desire to be independent, part of me really liked living at home. Until the rows started to get serious.

It started with my first car, the Vitara. Even though I couldn't yet drive I bought the Vitara from a friend of mine. I loved the idea of the car. It was cool, it was grown up and it was mine. The plan was that I would get my friend Ginnie, who had passed her test, to drive me to work each day and collect me after filming. She was pleased about this as she was at college at the time and couldn't afford her own car. Under this arrangement once she had chauffeured me to the set each morning she had use of the car for the rest of the day and I'd give her a bit of cash in exchange for her time. So it worked well for us both. But my Dad was not happy. It wasn't the car as such, more the fact that I had bought it, without any prior discussion with them, when I hadn't even passed my test. He tried to talk to me, but I wouldn't listen. I wanted it, so I was going to have it.

Seven months later, when I did pass my test, I traded the Vitara up for a BMW M3 convertible, and this time he was livid.

'You're going to get yourself killed!' he said to me when I showed it to him. 'That's the kind of car a thirty-year-old should have, not a teenage girl! The car you had before was fine! You are going to put yourself into an early coffin.'

'I can afford it,' I said.

'You work yourself towards something like that, Danni. You build yourself up to things in life. You don't just go and get them because you can! Life isn't like that.'

'Don't be ridiculous, she's just enjoying herself,' my mother said in my defence.

'Well, when we get a phone call at three in the morning saying she's been in a car crash, then maybe you'll listen,' he fumed.

My father was always the voice of reason in our

house, but more often than not my mother overrode him. Now that I was earning my own money I felt I could do the same. We had always been so close but we started to bicker. I gave him a lot of back-chat.

'You're living beyond your means, Danniella,' he'd say. 'You're still just a teenager!'

'It's my money. I'll spend it how I want,' was my standard refrain.

And with that I'd grab my car keys, storm out of the house, slamming the door, and drive off.

Despite the fact that she tended to side with me against my Dad in rows, my mother was also pretty sensible about money. She had been always very careful about investing my salary and giving me just enough to see me through. And she was always very fair if I asked for extra money. I remember once in the early days asking her whether she would advance me enough money for a Helen Storey dress. It was only £200 but it was the most expensive piece of clothing I had ever bought. I was going to a big work party, one of my first glamorous occasions, and I wanted to look right. I couldn't just go in a Lycra top and miniskirt, the kind of clothes I wore if I was going out in Loughton, and she understood this. Knowing that I wanted it and also needed it, she gave me the money without hesitation. She knew it was the right thing to do, and in any case it was *my* money. I had earned it fairly and squarely. If I wanted to spend £200 on one dress that that was my decision.

But once I started to model and do work outside of the show she had less control of my money. The fees I got from that work didn't go to Sylvia Young or to her. I would be paid direct and so I now had money with which to do what I wanted and buy what I liked, when I liked, which was how I was able to buy the BMW. And as I became more involved in the celebrity circuit I wanted to spend more and more money. I wanted to fit in, and to look and act the part, so I'd buy piles of designer clothes. I liked labels like John Richmond, Hyper Hyper, jeans and jackets from American Classics. None of it was very expensive but it was a lot for a girl my age and it set me apart from my contemporaries back home. I'd go on holidays – shopping trips to Paris, a week's break in Spain – and invite some of my old friends to come along too. If we went out at night I'd treat them all. If I had drunk too much to drive I'd think nothing of getting a cab from Essex to the West End. If I saw something in a shop that I wanted for my flat – a stereo, a TV, something like that – I'd buy it there and then. I never used to think about it first, sleep on it, work out whether I could afford it. I'd just get it. It used to upset my father so much.

'This is the worst thing that has happened to you, getting this job, Danniella,' he once said to me. 'You should have never have been an actress. You should have stayed at the stables and just been happy. This money is going to be your downfall.'

How right he was.

It was no longer just clothes and shoes and cars and holidays that I was spending my money on. By now I was buying drugs as well. It started off with me buying just a bit here and there. If I was going on a big evening out, to a club or some party, and there was a dealer around, I'd get some – just a gram to start with. I wouldn't take it all myself during the evening. I'd share it with people and sometimes if I didn't finish it then I'd have some left over for the next night out. During my first year on the soap I bought and took coke on a purely recreational basis, maybe once or, at a push, twice in eight weeks, and I never let it interfere with my work. I'd take it at the weekends or when I wasn't working. But by the time I was seventeen my drug use had become much more frequent.

It was mainly to do with this new social scene in which I was moving. You see, in that world a 'big night out' didn't mean just going out at the weekend. On that scene there was a big night out to be had every night of the week if you wanted it. I wouldn't say that it was a particularly druggy scene. The places that I went to were classy and sophisticated bars and clubs. Nor did they, as far as I am aware, condone the use of drug taking on their premises. But amongst the crowd I was socialising with drug taking was commonplace. A lot of people – quite normal people – took drugs, whether they were smoking spliff, taking ecstasy or doing coke. You were never made to feel that you had to partake, but if you did it certainly wasn't frowned upon.

Over time, as I went out more and more, I took and bought more and more cocaine. That's how the ball got rolling. I'd go to a party and think it was quite normal for me to have a line of coke, just as I would have thought, a year earlier, about ordering a vodka, lime and soda if I was out with the girls at a bar. I took coke because I was out, because I wanted to, because I was having a good time and it made me feel great. I still didn't really understand all the negative fuss about coke. I didn't see that there was any harm in it, and I was never reprimanded for it. No one took me aside and said, 'You've got a problem.'

But I did have a problem, even then, and although this may sound strange, it wasn't so much with the drug itself because, frankly, it could have been any other poison. The problem was with my inability to draw the line, to know when to stop. Over the years I have met many people who have taken cocaine and not become addicted to it, just as I have many friends who enjoy a glass of wine but are not alcoholics. But I'm not one of those people. If I had a line, I soon wanted another, then another. If I was having a good time, I wanted the night to last for ever. And if I had a good night out during the week, then I'd want to do it all over again, just days later – and the fact is, because I had money, I could afford to. I could have as much fun and take as much coke as I wanted. There was nothing stopping me. Certainly, nothing inside me. I had no self-control, no discipline.

One night, towards the end of my second year on the soap, for the first time in ages I went out with the girls from home. We hadn't planned to have a big night out as such. We went to a couple of bars, then to a club where we danced for hours. The girls had their vodka, lime and sodas and I had mine, along with a little something else, which I had stashed away in my pocket, and would take at regular intervals in the loo. When the club closed in the early hours of the morning, we headed off to get something to eat. The girls were tired and hungry. I, of course, having snorted the best part of a gram of Charlie up my nose, on my own, was anything but.

'Oh, come on!' I said to them. 'Don't be such lightweights! Forget the food, let's go somewhere else and have a drink.'

I stood on the pavement and tried to hail a cab.

'What?' said Ginnie. 'Have you gone mad? You must be insane. It's three in the morning. We're all tired, we need to sleep.'

'Oh come on! Don't be so fucking boring,' I said. 'Let's go. I know somewhere that's still open!'

Ginnie turned on me. 'Danni, what's your problem these days? Why are you like this? Why can't you be like you used to be? Why can't you be like the rest of us? Why can't you just have a good night out, get a kebab and then go home? What's happened to you?'

What had happened to me was that, even though I didn't realise it then, I had already become addicted to cocaine.

6

WEST END GIRL

....

'Be careful who you are friends with,' Ross had said to me. 'Try and keep them about you. Beware of people who lull you into a false sense of security. There will be people who want to befriend you just because of who you are, be very aware of that.' Wise words, indeed, and ones I'd often think of later, but which fell on very deaf ears at the time.

I didn't see much of the girls again following my row with Ginnie in the street that night. I kept in contact with Ginnie and we would speak on the phone from time to time, but I stopped socialising with them. Looking back now, I can see that it was a mutual decision. They didn't like what I had become and I didn't like who they still were. In my mind they were unsophisticated, petty, provincial and boring. If they wanted to remain like that for the rest of their lives, then so be it. But I wasn't going to end up like that. I wasn't going to spend my entire life in the wine bars of

Essex. There was a whole new, bigger and better world to be had, one they didn't know about. But I had seen it and liked it, and I wanted to be part of it.

The fact that I had suddenly lost all my friends from home, some of whom I had known since early childhood, didn't bother me in the slightest, for I didn't see it as a problem at the time. It never really occurred to me then that it was as much their decision as it was mine. I convinced myself that it had been my choice to stop being friends with them. What I didn't realise was that they could no longer put up with me. They still loved me but they just couldn't cope with me any more. I was too much of a liability. We no longer lived the same lives or shared the same outlook. My behaviour, fuelled by my dependence on cocaine, had seen to that. But who needed them anyway, I reckoned.

And so I went and broke what is, perhaps, the most cardinal rule on how to live your life when you become famous: I ditched my old friends, the ones who had known and loved me before I was famous, the ones I had grown up with, the ones who kept me grounded, who knew me for the person I really was. I went up West and within a matter of days had found myself a whole new group of instant playmates to have fun with.

It is amazingly easy to make new friends when you are well known. People can't wait to meet you, to include you in their group, to make you feel like one of them. They can't help themselves. You only have to be in their company for a couple of minutes before they are buying you drinks, giving you their numbers, taking you into their confidence, showering you with compliments and anointing you as their new best friend. But, of course, the great paradox of this is that you are anything but. They are not real friends at all. They don't really care about you, as I was to discover later on. They care about you, as Ross said, just for *what* are you, not *who* you are, deep down, within. But none of this occurred to me then. I was far too young and naïve to see it that way, and in any case, at the age of seventeen, *I* didn't really know who I was yet.

I found my new friends out and about in the bars and clubs of the West End, and I thought to myself, these are my kind of people. They weren't celebrities as such but they moved in that world. They were older than I was, they were glamorous and sophisticated, and best of all they knew how to have a good time. There was no going home early for them because of college the next day. No 'I can't come out mid week because of work.' And certainly no 'I'm staying in tonight because I'm broke.' These people, my new friends, made none of these excuses, because they didn't have to. They had success-ful jobs but they knew how to balance work and play. They had money, so they could always afford to party and be spontaneous. And they thought nothing of going out every night of the week, because that was their world, their *raison d'être*.

And it soon became mine as well. It wasn't long before I started to go out with them in central London maybe two or three times during the week as well as at weekends. We'd go to parties, big club nights, and hang out in the bars of the moment. Because most of this crowd belonged to private members' clubs, the night didn't end at normal pub closing time. When time was called we'd head off to a private club until about two or three in the morning, then I'd head home, hitting my pillow about an hour later.

It was an adventure, it was fun. And all this time I was doing coke. It was no longer something to do at the weekend, or on a special occasion. I'd take coke every single time I went out, sometimes three or four times a week.

I would have said, if you had asked me at the time, that I was still using the drug recreationally, because that is what it seemed like to me. I was taking coke when I was out and having a laugh. I wasn't taking it during the day, and I wasn't taking it at work. There were days when I didn't even touch the stuff at all. I did it to have fun, to unwind, to give myself a buzz. I did it for pleasure, to have a good time. The trouble was, these good times were becoming all too frequent. Taking cocaine three or four times a week is by no means recreational use: that is what you call a serious habit, a dependency, and mine was now so bad that I couldn't contemplate going out for the evening without using it.

The drug made me feel great. It gave me confidence and made me sparky and chatty. When I was tired from a day's work it gave me the energy to go out that night. When I walked into a room for the first time, being on cocaine gave me that boost I needed. I felt truly alive, I felt amazing. Who would want to feel anything but?

The buzz you get from the first line of cocaine of the evening doesn't last very long, maybe twenty minutes at a push, and so I would take line after line throughout the night, chasing that initial high. If we were out in a public place I was always discreet. I'd make my excuses, go to the Ladies, take out my wrap and cut myself a line on the lid of the loo seat and snort it through a banknote. I would do this at regular intervals in the way that another girl might reapply her make-up.

If I was at a private party with my friends I wouldn't think twice about doing it in front of them. Unlike my friends back home this new crowd didn't have any scruples about such things. Why should they? They were all doing it too. You could always guarantee if you were out with that group that someone would have something on them and they'd be more than willing to give you a bit if you didn't have any.

But by now this was no longer a risk I was prepared to take. I couldn't rely on bumping into a dealer and scoring at a bar or club. I always made sure that I had my own, that I was carrying. Before I went out at night

I'd make the call to my dealer and see if they would deliver it to me. When I was still living at home I'd have to tell my parents that they were just friends of mine, but when I moved into my flat at the age of eighteen that was no longer an issue. If the dealer couldn't come to me then I would go to them and pick it up on my way into town. Doing this not only ensured that I had my own supply of drugs, but also meant that I could have a line before I went out and that I'd be in the right frame of mind when I arrived at my destination. I must have had the names and numbers of about three or four dealers in my book then. I'd have a couple that covered the Loughton area and a couple up town. You see, you could never just rely on one. What if they weren't around? What if they couldn't make the delivery on time? What if you ran out of gear while you were up West and your dealer was miles away back at home? You always had to have back-up.

It is exactly this kind of thought pattern that separates the recreational user from the addict. A recreational user might think: 'Wouldn't it be fun to take some coke if it was there?' But if they can't get their hands on some, fail to score, it's not the end of the world. They will carry on and party anyway, putting the whole idea of taking drugs to the back of their mind, and have a good time without them. But for anyone who is drug dependent in any way it's not like that. When you want it, you *have* to have it, no matter what lengths you need to go to, no matter how much it costs you. You will drive to the ends of the earth if need be to get your little kick. It becomes a mission, an obsession, a nagging hunger that eats away at you, something you can't get out of your mind until you have had it. I couldn't have imagined, by that stage, going out without taking drugs. To me the two things had become synonymous. There was no pleasure to be derived from simply going out and getting something to eat with people you knew or from having a nice chat with a friend over a couple of glasses of wine. Going out meant taking coke. Actually, I think it got to the stage for me where it was no longer clear which came first. Was I taking coke because I was going out? Or was I going out in order just to take coke? By then those lines had blurred.

Most seventeen-year-olds wouldn't be able to get away with this kind of behaviour or lifestyle. Unless they were working in the world that I was or had access to a large private income there is no way they would have been able to afford the life I was leading. Even if you take the money I was spending on drugs out of the equation, that lifestyle was hugely expensive. At the bars and clubs I went to a drink could set you back ten or twenty pounds. Then there were all the cab fares, club entrance fees and the clothes – because you didn't get to hang out in that world unless you looked the part. Of course, a lot of the time, simply because I was well known, I was able to blag it.

Doormen at clubs would let me in for free because they wanted a 'face' for the evening, strange men would buy me drinks at a bar to show off to their friends, and clothes shops would give me discounts on the off chance that I would be photographed wearing their labels. Even so, I was still spending a lot of money but it didn't matter, it didn't worry me, because I had it.

Once the work was finished on my flat and I had moved into it my parents had no control over me. They couldn't tell me to stay in or advise me to have an early night or get my beauty sleep. Since I wasn't living with them, they had no idea what I was up to. Sure, they knew that I was going out a lot in the evening, but they didn't know what time I was getting home, who I was mixing with or that I was buying and taking an illegal Class A drug on a regular basis. If they had known they would have been horrified.

Thanks to my income I was now in possession of two key accessories that played a role in my downfall – my flat and my car. The flat gave me the privacy I needed to live this life. If a dealer delivered drugs to me that was fine. I didn't have to give anyone an explanation as to who this person was or what he or she was doing in my flat. The car was another tool. It meant that I could get around London easily and collect drugs if I wanted to. Both these things made it easier for me to lead my double life.

I didn't have any problems with work either, at least initially. During that year I was able to juggle my social life with the working day. The producers and directors appreciated the fact that the younger members of the cast liked to go out and party, and we were never discouraged from doing so just as long as we got to work on time and behaved professionally on set. There was plenty of time when we weren't filming during the day to sit and learn our lines, so I didn't have any problem in that respect. If we did have a big night and were a bit tired the next day, they and the older members of the cast would just tease us. As far as the producers were concerned I wasn't acting any differently from Sid or Michelle – but in fact of course I was. They still saw me as a fresh-faced teenager from Loughton who was having a good time, and for a while I was able to get away with it. Being so young, even if I had stayed up late at night drinking and taking drugs, I didn't really feel the effects of it the next day. I didn't get hangovers then. I could survive on a few hours' sleep and still roll into work the next day and do my job.

And then there were my friends or, rather, the lack of them. With Ginnie and co out of the picture I had no one in my life to take me aside and say, 'Do you think you should be doing that?' or to tell me to keep a lid on it. And that's the way I liked it. In my new social circle no one would have thought twice about how I was behaving because that's the way they lived their lives too. I was managing it all quite well. I thought: 'I can handle this, I'm in control.' And for a time I was. But the problem was, because I had no one to answer to, because there was nothing holding me back, things soon began to escalate, to the point where I seemed to have entered a whole new dimension.

At around the age of eighteen, after a year of living this way, I fell in with a group of people from South London. I had met them on the club scene and we'd bump into each other once or twice a week. They seemed perfectly nice to me. OK, I grant you, they weren't the type of people I would have invited back to my parents' house for tea but, in a sense, that is exactly why I liked them. There was something gritty and raw about this group of people. They were cool and streetwise and had an air of danger about them, which excited me. I think I was trying subconsciously to escape from my own squeaky-clean, girl-next-door image. Now that I was older I wanted people to see me differently. I wanted to be someone else, something I wasn't. I wanted to have an edge, and I believed that by being with these people I could have that.

Unlike my West End friends, these people didn't have glamorous jobs. They weren't club owners or DJs, or in showbusiness, fashion or anything like that. They worked, yes, and they made money too – but none of them held down what my father would have regarded as an honest, proper job. They were people who knew how to work the system. They were dealers

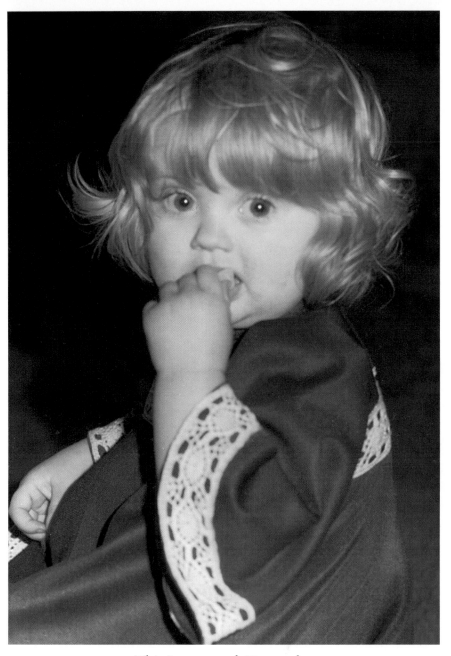

This is me, aged 18 months.
Shame I'm wearing my mum's curtains!

You can tell I took school seriously!

I'm 13 in this photo, which was taken for Spotlight, the casting directory. I was always in a desperate hurry to grow up.

Outside the Sylvia Young Theatre School, in my school uniform.

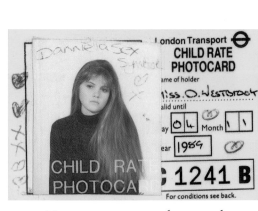

Not your average photocard shot. Who did I think I was?

My first day at *EastEnders*, in those denim hotpants.

This was my very first *EastEnders* publicity shoot. I was 16.

When I got the part of Sam Mitchell I knew that all the hard work for that Grade 8 acting exam had paid off!

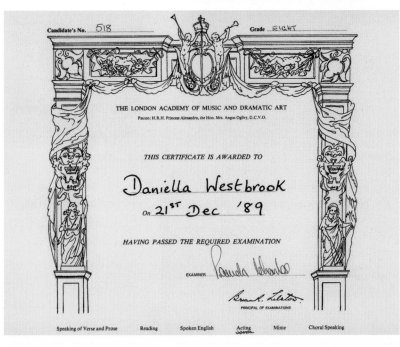

Candidate's No. 518   Grade EIGHT

THE LONDON ACADEMY OF MUSIC AND DRAMATIC ART

Patron: H.R.H. Princess Alexandra, the Hon. Mrs. Angus Ogilvy, G.C.V.O.

THIS CERTIFICATE IS AWARDED TO

Daniella Westbrook

On 21ST Dec '89

HAVING PASSED THE REQUIRED EXAMINATION

EXAMINER

PRINCIPAL OF EXAMINATIONS

Speaking of Verse and Prose   Reading   Spoken English   Acting   Mime   Choral Speaking

A shoot for the *News of the World...* in ski-pants?!

Another photo shoot with Jeany Savage, glamour photographer *extraordinaire...* This one was for the *Daily Star*.

DANNIELLA WESTBROOK
EastEnders' Sexiest Star

Voted Sexiest Star, not that there was a prize - this was in the days before there was an awards ceremony for the opening of an envelope.

Mum, me and Daddy
at my eighteenth
birthday party.

Turning 18 with the lovely
Gillian Taylforth.

The vodka, lime and soda girls
out on the town . . . What *am*
I wearing?!

On holiday in
Thailand with my
friend Claire.

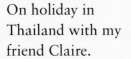

On set with the man who put the 'M' in 'Mitchell' – Ross Kemp, my biggest brother.

Me and Mike Reid. A real diamond geezer, a real straight-talker and, man, what a golfer!

Another *EastEnders* publicity shot with Sid Owen. We were like the poor man's Posh and Becks . . .

Back on set and hard at work watching the scene we'd just filmed.

Racing at Silverstone, being a diva!
Where's my Ferrari?

Leaving Brown's nightclub with Ross.
You can tell he was worried and that I
was not well.

On set with the genius that is Timothy Spall and the legendary
Lesley Sharp. I played moody teenager Dawn Stubbs.

Leaving rehab for the first time. It was obvious I didn't get it – check out the outfit and the Chanel bag. In denial, clearly . . .

Back to reality - yet another night out at Brown's. And I thought this was fun – how wrong can you be?

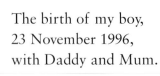

The birth of my boy, 23 November 1996, with Daddy and Mum.

and thieves, bank robbers and gangsters. In short, they belonged to the underworld.

Why did I want to be with them? I was, after all, a nicely brought up, privately educated, middle-class girl from the suburbs. And even if I didn't have a posh accent I had been raised to know right from wrong, to be courteous and kind at all times and to mind my p's and q's. I suppose, looking back at that time, it was really just another act of rebellion. All my life I had been cocooned in this comfortable little world, which I was now desperate to escape from. And there was something compelling about these people, something about their air of disregard, their hardness and their devil-may-care attitude. I was, for some incredibly strange reason, impressed by them.

These people in turn were impressed by me and I liked that. They thought I was something special – to start with, at least. They liked the fact that I was famous, that I had money. In Loughton such things had never really mattered to my friends. Because they had known me from such a young age my fame didn't impress them. If anything it went the other way, because they were always trying to keep my feet on the ground and remind me of who I really was. Nor did they care about my money. As far as they were concerned it was nice when I was able to treat them to a present or a holiday, but it was never the linchpin of our friendship, it was entirely incidental. Very little, to their credit, ever impressed those girls. But with this crowd it was different. They liked having a famous friend and treated me accordingly, and I enjoyed it. I liked the attention, the respect and all that came with it.

This crowd went to the same bars and club nights that I went to with my West End friends. That's where I'd see them, and after a while we became friends. I'd drink with them, have a dance and a laugh and would take drugs with them. But unlike my West End friends, who ended their evening when the private members' club finally shut in the early hours of the morning, this group would carry on partying. As they didn't have jobs to go to, and therefore didn't have to be up in the morning, they could drink and do drugs all night if they wanted to. This was appealing to me. When I was as high as a kite at three in the morning the last thing I wanted to do was go to bed. I wanted to carry on, and so when one of this South London crew asked me at a night club if I wanted to go on with them to a bar when the club shut, I said, 'Yeah! Why not?'

We ended up in an illegal, after-hours drinking club in South London. It was sleazy and grim and full of unsavoury-looking people, but that just added to the thrill of it. I thought I had seen it all but I had never been to a place like this before. I felt that I had crossed the line and entered the underworld, and that excited me. We stayed up most of the night, drinking, talking, taking drugs, and by the time I stumbled out of that bar it was already light, the birds were singing, and people were starting to make their way to work. As my evening was coming to an end, their day was just beginning. But rather than feeling anxious about that, or being concerned that I hadn't gone to sleep yet, I thought: 'This is great, this is fantastic.' I'd finally met some people who had as much stamina as I had. People who had the same desire to live life, not let it pass them by.

And so I began to hang out with these people more and more. I'd see them out on the town, at clubs and parties, and more often than not, a couple of nights a week, we would all end up in these bars – or spills, as they are called – doing our thing.

The irony is that although I thought at the time that I had formed great friendships within this group, the only thing we really had in common was our love of drugs. That's what held us together. I can't recall ever having a meaningful conversation with any of them, I was too far gone for that, and it is a well-known fact that cocaine users talk a lot of rubbish when they are on the drug anyway. But at the time that didn't bother me. Our one shared interest was enough for me – so long as they used I was happy to spend all my time with them.

As I saw more and more of this group my cocaine use rapidly began to spiral out of control. When I had been hanging out with my West End crowd my drug consumption had been frequent and by most people's standards extreme, but it was nothing to the amounts I started to take now that I was mixing with this new crowd. When I was involved with the West End scene I would buy a maximum of maybe two or three grams of coke a week. Back then I only used the drug when I was out. I was coming home at two or three in the morning, so there was a limit to how much I took in an evening. And there would be several days each week when I stayed in for the evening. On those occasions I not only didn't take coke but didn't even think about it.

But as I became more involved with this South London set things changed. Because I was now staying up till dawn I was taking more and more coke each night. I found myself taking and buying twice as much as I used to, sometimes even more. I was going out four times a week, and often these nights were back to back. It became quite commonplace to go out of an evening and not go to sleep – and then do it all again the following night. Wednesday, Thursday, Friday, Saturday . . . it was relentless, and the only way to survive and keep up with this set was to carry on using, to take more and more of the drug.

The more coke I took, the more heavily I drank. If you are out from eight in the evening till eight the next morning, that's a good twelve hours of drinking time. But I wasn't just drinking when I was out, I'd drink at home too when I was staying in. I loved champagne and always made sure I had a couple of bottles of it in the fridge – Dom Pérignon, Laurent-Perrier Rosé and

Bollinger were my favourites. I'd think nothing of coming home from work in the evening and opening a bottle of champagne even if I was on my own. I'd sit down, turn the telly on and down the bottle within just a couple of hours. Sometimes if I wanted to get really hammered I'd pour a shot of vodka into the glass to spice up the mix.

It goes without saying that this lifestyle had a dramatic effect on my personality and my relationships with other people. I experienced violent mood swings as I went from high to low and back again. Lack of sleep caused me to be both irritable and irrational. I could be snappy, over-emotional, hotheaded, often lashing out at the people who were nearest and dearest to me. For two years I had successfully managed to hide my drug problem from my family, but once I started moving with the South London set it became obvious to my parents that there was something wrong.

It was, in fact, my mother who realised that it was drugs. Working at the Valbonne club in the Seventies she had seen that world, she had seen people on drugs and she knew what it did to them, how it affected them. And as she saw me metamorphose from a bubbly, vivacious teenager into this paranoid, angry, moody shadow of my former self, alarm bells began to ring. I was not behaving as I normally did.

When I was mixing with the West End crowd, even after I'd left home, I was still very family minded. If I wasn't going out in the evening I'd often pop round to my parents' house and have a cup of tea with them and Jay after work, and I never missed our family lunch on Sunday, whatever I had been up to the night before. I loved those moments together. I felt secure and happy there; it was a place I could retreat to and be myself.

But once I started mixing with this new set and taking more and more drugs my attitude changed. I'd go round to my parents' house and be abusive. I'd answer back, taking my aggression out on Mum and Dad. I started skipping Sunday lunch, sometimes because I was just too tired and was sleeping off the night before, on other occasions because I wanted to be with my new friends instead. Rather than sit down to a delicious lunch with people who loved and cared for me, I'd be out with them, scoring and taking drugs. Sometimes I'd call my parents to tell them I wasn't coming, sometimes I just didn't bother to show up.

When my mother confronted me about my lifestyle I just denied it.

'What do you know about my life?' I'd sneer. 'What do you care?'

When she told me that it was exactly because she cared that she was having to have this conversation with me in the first place, I'd tell her where to go.

'Oh, shut up, you miserable old cow,' I'd shout at her. 'You know nothing about me or my friends!'

I find it difficult to write those words now. I can't

quite believe that I could have said those things to her, that I could have caused her so much pain. If one of my children spoke to me like that I would be beside myself, I am not sure how I would cope. But she was always so strong, she always stood up to me, even though I know now how frightened she was for me inside.

She was at the end of her tether and arranged for me to pay a visit to one of my local GPs to discuss my problems. However, she knew that I wouldn't go on my own and that I certainly wouldn't go with her, so she asked my father to take me. She knew that if anyone was going to get me down to the surgery then it would be him. If she had told me she was taking me there I would have refused point blank and told her where to go, but with my father it was different. Because I listened to him and respected him, I would do it for him, and so the poor man was forced to take me to the appointment. We spent most of the car journey in silence, not knowing what to say to each other. He was consumed with worry and hurt, I was embarrassed and upset that I had let him down. Of course, I didn't say that to him at the time. I was still in denial.

It was a pointless exercise. I was surly and unco-operative during the appointment and the doctor just didn't want to know.

'It's up to her what she wants to do with her life,' he told my father after the consultation.

He didn't suggest that I should get help; he didn't refer me to see a psychiatrist or recommend that I attend a local meeting of Narcotics Anonymous. He said nothing. He didn't even proffer any advice or write me a prescription. He just closed the door on me. And so I continued on my own personal journey down that all too slippery road to self-destruction.

7

GOING OFF THE RAILS

....

My dependency on cocaine not only had a profound effect on my friendships but on my love life as well. You see, when you are seriously addicted to anything, whether it's drugs, drink or gambling, for example, it is hard to establish a proper, meaningful relationship with anyone because your addiction will always come first. And that's how it was with me.

In the course of my late teens and my early twenties I had a number of boyfriends, but none of these relationships was particularly serious for, as much as it shames me to admit to this, my first and greatest love then was always cocaine. I can see now that my relationship with the drug came before any boy or man I was involved with during those years. It affected how I was with them, how I behaved, how we were together as a couple. It sometimes even determined who I went out with. During those years I first dated a boy from my area I had known for some time, then an actor, a member of a boy band who I was with for several years, and later I had a short relationship with one of my South London set.

I am not trying to write any of these relationships off. At the time I thought they were all special and wonderful, but now that I am older and wiser I can see them for what they were. I can safely say I was never really in love with any of them and, if I am honest, I don't believe that any of them truly loved me either. Like any other girl I made my fair share of mistakes and I always seemed to be falling for the wrong type of person. I wouldn't say that it was solely down to my drug addiction, but I believe that cocaine did cloud my judgement a lot of the time.

I made a decision a long time ago never to talk about my past relationships in detail. It's not helpful to the people I went out with, it's not helpful to me and it certainly isn't helpful to anyone else. An important element of my recovery has been to accept responsibility for my own actions and for my addiction. Of course, over the years I had boyfriends who witnessed me take drugs, and there were some, but by no means all, who used with me. But not one of my boyfriends was responsible for the way I turned out, and I will never let them be blamed for it. That was down to me. If any of them had tried to stop me from using I would have walked away from the relationship – just as I had done with my friends. If someone didn't like the way that I behaved then that was too bad, I just wouldn't

see them any more. If they said something that I didn't
want to hear, I wouldn't talk to them.

It was the same with my family. After the trip to the
doctor's surgery I avoided my parents for a while, keen
to avoid another of their 'interventions'. If Justin, who
I had always looked up to, commented on my drug
taking I'd ignore him for days on end. One by one I
began to shut them all out. I isolated myself from the
people who wanted to help me, and that's when my
addiction began to reach really dangerous levels.

In 1993, after three years of working on *EastEnders*, I
decided to leave the soap. My contract was up for
renewal and I thought it was time for me to move on. I
had been offered a part in a new ITV comedy drama
called *Frank Stubbs Promotes*, starring alongside Timothy Spall and Leslie Sharpe, and I decided that it
would be good for me to make the break and try
something new while I still had youth on my side. As
much as I enjoyed being in *EastEnders* and liked the
security of working on a soap opera, I was also well
aware of the fact that I was in danger of becoming
type-cast for ever if I carried on playing Sam. The
producers didn't have a problem with me leaving. It
was felt that my character had done as much as she
could in the space of three years, anyway. During that
time Sam had, after all, been involved in a story about
under-age sex, run off to Gretna Green to marry
Ricky, been evicted from her home, become a squatter,

tried her luck as a topless model, fought on a regular basis with her brothers Grant and Phil, and gone through a marriage break-up. I think we all agreed that the poor girl was in need of a break, and so the writers sent her off to work on a cruise liner. In January 1993 I filmed my final scenes and Sam Mitchell, in true *EastEnders* style, waved goodbye to Albert Square from the back of a London taxi cab.

Many people assume that the first time I left the soap I did so under a cloud, but in fact nothing could have been further from the truth. Although the producers agreed that it was the right time for my character to move on, they wanted to keep the door open for her to return at a later date, as they knew how popular the Mitchell family were with the viewers. I was really pleased that they decided not to kill the character off, not only as it gave me the option to return if things didn't go to plan, but also because I liked working there. The cast and crew had become my second family and I didn't like the thought of never seeing or working with any of them again.

Although I had been taking a lot of drugs during that final year on the soap, I don't think anyone on set was aware that I had a problem. I had successfully managed to conceal my drug taking from them all, so it was not an issue when I left. During that period I never took drugs at work and never had them with me when I was on set. Even when I was doing the West End and South London scene and having a big night out, if I had to be at work the next day I always managed to get some sleep before I went to work. If I was tired during the day I would take a short nap in my dressing-room, which no one minded about. So long as you were around to rehearse and do your scene, and on time for hair and make-up and costume fittings, no one really cared what you were up to in your free time – they were too busy to notice.

As soon as I started work on *Frank Stubbs* – just a week after leaving *EastEnders* – I knew that I had made the right decision about my career. My character Dawn was very different from Sam, and that was good for me, because for too long I had played that role as if I was on autopilot. I liked working with new people too – not just Tim and Leslie, who are great actors, but with a different director and crew as well. They worked us hard there. It wasn't like *EastEnders*, where you could sit around for days with nothing to do because you weren't involved in a story-line. We worked solidly for six months, and when we were shooting we worked day and night. It was tough but I enjoyed it. It was all so refreshing and new and I began to believe that I had a future away from the soap, that I would be able to cross that bridge and move on, and for a while it looked as though I was going to. The show was met with good reviews, a second series was commissioned and it wasn't long before I was being offered more parts, such as a role in an art movie directed by Dave Stewart.

But the problem I faced wasn't to do with work – it was more a question of what to do when I wasn't working. When I stopped shooting *Frank Stubbs* I found myself with time on my hands. Being on *East-Enders* had been like having a full-time job. Whether you were in a scene or not you still had to go to work every day. But suddenly I had all this time on my hands. I was beginning to see what it was like for other actors. There would be weeks, months even when you had nothing to do because you were in between jobs, or waiting to film another series. And that wasn't good for me.

When *Frank Stubbs* came to an end after two seasons I was effectively out of work. It was 1994, a year after I had left *EastEnders*. Of course, I should have spent the time I was 'resting', as they say in theatre land when your work dries up, doing exactly that. I should have been taking care of myself and using that time to pursue other projects, read scripts and go to auditions. In other words, I should have treated those periods as though I was still working, but instead I stupidly behaved as though I was on an extended holiday. I went out, partied and had a good time. Without the routine of working life there was even less reason not to have a late night; with nothing to do during the day I could stay up until the morning if I wanted to and, more often than not, I did. And there was also nothing to stop me now from taking drugs. I could take as many as I wanted – and sure enough, true to form, I did.

It was a vicious circle. The more free time I had, the more I went out. And the more I went out, the more drugs I took. And the more drugs I took the less inclined I was to work. And so it went on. My agent, Sylvia, would call from time to time with offers of work but I really wasn't interested. I just wanted to have a good time, and the problem was I could afford to. I still had a lot money left from *EastEnders, Frank Stubbs* and my modelling work. I had sold my flat in Woodford the year before and I was able to buy a penthouse flat in a luxury gated complex in Buckhurst Hill, in Essex. So I didn't really have any financial incentive to go back to work. I went on like this for a year, during which the only work I agreed to do was the odd modelling job.

By the time I reached the age of twenty-one I would say that my addiction had become very serious. With no job to keep me on the straight and narrow I was using the drug every day of the week. I now couldn't actually go a day without using cocaine and was doing as much as an eighth of an ounce a day, which is around three and a half grams of the drug. You'd buy an eighth, or an eight ball as it is sometimes called, from your dealer, because it made – wait for this – more financial sense. An eighth cost £150, so at £50 a gram you got that little bit extra for free. I know it sounds crazy, but when you were buying as much as I did then these things mattered. So by taking an eighth a day I was now not only doing as much coke in one day as I used to in an entire week when I was with my West End friends, but I was also spending over £1,000 a week on my habit. More than £50,000 a year.

By now I was going out five or six nights of the week and I wasn't just doing the club scene either. When the clubs closed I'd sit up most of the night in the spills with my underworld friends, and when we weren't doing that I'd be back at one of their flats in South London. I didn't mind where I was – it no longer mattered to me. So long as I had my coke then I couldn't have cared less where I was or who was with me.

Sometimes I did as much as four to five grams a day, and my drug taking was no longer confined to evening sessions now. With nothing to do during the day I wouldn't think twice about having a little pick-me-up in the middle of the afternoon and would carry on like this until I went out at night, when, of course, I would take even more. Because of the drug I wasn't eating or sleeping properly, and when I managed to get to bed I would do so at strange times of day, for hours on end. By now my body was so weak, so worn down, that I found it hard to do the most basic of tasks.

One morning during this period I went to take a bath and then found that I couldn't get out of it. I simply didn't have the strength within me. I was too weak and frail. I was so thin by then that sitting in the bath was uncomfortable. The bones in my bottom were now so pronounced that there was nothing to cushion my body from the porcelain of the tub, and I didn't have enough strength in my arms to push my body out of it. I started to panic.

I still had one friend left from my old life, my brother's former girlfriend Janice, with whom I had entrusted a key to the place in case of an emergency. Fortunately that morning I had taken my mobile into the bathroom with me and so was able to call her from there.

'You've got to help me,' I cried.

'What on earth is the matter?'

'I just can't manage it, I can't do it, Janice. I can't get out of the bath. You've got to come and help me.'

Within the space of twenty minutes Janice had let herself into the flat and was in the bathroom lifting my cold, frail, naked body out of the bath.

'I can feel my bones,' I wept. 'I can feel my bones.'

As I stood there on the bath mat trying to dry myself with a towel, Janice was shocked by my appearance. I was so thin you could see every rib and every bone down the back of my spine.

My psychological state was not much better than my physical one. I suffered from terrible bouts of depression, which were sometimes so bad that I couldn't move from the flat. I just didn't have the will or the energy. This was coupled with a deep and often irrational sense of paranoia. I believed that people were out to get me, or that the police were about to turn up at the flat and arrest me. When I was alone in the apartment I wouldn't answer the door to anyone unless I knew who they were. If someone turned up out of the blue and rang the bell I was far too scared just to answer the intercom. I wouldn't even open the door to my dealer, which is really saying something. When he called round I would buzz him through the intercom, once I knew for sure it was him, and let him through the main door of the building, but once he got to my front door I wouldn't open it. Instead I'd push the money I owed him through the letterbox and he would push back an envelope filled with my supply. When he was gone I'd tape up the letterbox, so that not even the postman could see through it.

During that year I had very little contact with anyone except my dealers and a couple of my friends from South London. I lost all contact with my *East-Enders* friends and didn't even see Sid. I never let my parents come round to the flat and I rarely went to visit them. I didn't want them to see me like that, as I knew what their reaction would be. The sight of me would destroy my father, and I felt sure that my mother would try and put me into rehab and I didn't want to go.

My parents were, in fact, well aware of the gravity of the situation, because Janice had been keeping them informed. Because I refused to see them she was the only point of contact they still had with me. When she told them how concerned she was for my health after she had helped me out of the bath, they decided that somehow they must get me into a treatment centre – the question was how. They knew I wouldn't go with them, so their only hope was Janice.

And so one morning Janice called me to say that her grandmother had been taken sick. She said she wanted to visit her and asked me if I would come for moral support. Janice knew that this was the only way she could get me to leave the flat. I wouldn't have gone otherwise, but I knew how close she was to her Nan.

'Please come,' she said to me on the phone. 'It will be good for you anyway. It will take your mind off things for a while.'

It was May 1995. Janice arrived at the flat in the early afternoon. As I was getting my things together, trying to find my keys, my wallet – and drugs – she quickly went into my bedroom and packed a tiny bag for me with my nightwear, some underwear and my washbag. I was so out of it that I didn't even notice. We got into her car and drove off. I remember thinking that it was quite good fun, going on a road trip with Janice, and I was giggling and chatting away to her. I pulled out a wrap of coke from my jacket pocket and started cutting some lines out on the back of a packet of cigarettes. She gave me a sideways glance.

'What?' I laughed. 'What's wrong? Here, you have one!'

Janice couldn't believe it. This was something that

people did on a Friday night once in a while; they didn't do it in the middle of the week at three in the afternoon.

'Go on, have a bit,' I said, thrusting the cigarette packet towards her.

'No! I don't want one and you shouldn't either – it's Tuesday afternoon, for goodness sake!'

I didn't care what day of the week it was, or what time, and carried on using throughout the rest of the car journey. After about forty minutes we pulled up outside a hospital building in Marylebone, not far from where I had been to school. I looked around. There was a sign outside the building which read: 'The Nightingale Hospital'.

'Come on,' said Janice, grabbing the bag from the back of the car. 'Let's go.'

I got out of the car and followed her into the building. In the reception area there was another sign which read: 'Drug Rehabilitation Unit'.

I was confused and then burst out laughing.

'Why's your Nan in rehab?'

I couldn't get over the idea of Janice's granny being in rehab. It was the funniest thing I had ever heard.

But she wasn't smiling. She wasn't sharing the joke. 'She's not,' she said.

And then it dawned on me, and my world came crashing down. How could she do this to me? How could she lie like that? I started freaking out, kicking and screaming, trying to beat her up, swearing at her.

A nurse grabbed me, wrapped his arms round my body to hold me back and then sedated me.

When I came round I was lying in a hospital bed in a small room. I grabbed the phone on the bedside table and called my agent. I didn't really have anyone else left to speak to – I wasn't going to call my parents, as they had obviously put Janice up to this, and I certainly wasn't going to call her. 'Come here now,' I screamed at her. 'Come and get me out of here. They're trying to lock me up. They're trying to kill me!' She refused and put down the phone. I was furious, and in my rage I tried to smash up the room. I wasn't staying there, I wasn't going into treatment. I wasn't going to be treated like this, like some kind of animal. I was getting out of there.

I should have stayed at the hospital for at least a month, but after just a week in treatment I checked out. It was a hellish seven days. I hated the routine of the clinic, the treatment and the counselling, and I hated being away from cocaine. I hated Janice and my parents for what they had done and refused to speak to them while I was there. And so one evening when no one was looking I grabbed my bag, walked out of the hospital into the street and hailed a cab, instructing the driver to take me home.

My week's stay in rehab may not have cured my drug addiction but it paid off in other ways. Back in February of that year the press had got wind of the fact that I was addicted to cocaine, and the *Sunday Mirror* had rung my agent to say that they were going to run an exposé on me. Fortunately they had given her the opportunity to strike a deal with them. If I agreed to go on the record about it, and give them an interview filled with juicy quotes about my problems, they would go easy on me. And so back in February I had agreed to do my first 'cocaine shame' story. The paper printed a nice article about how I 'vowed to get clean' and said they were right behind me. I don't think anyone was that surprised by the news. Whilst few people were aware of the extent of my problems, it was a known fact that I liked to party and, frankly, there had been enough pictures printed of me stumbling out of clubs and bars in the past for people to realise that I must be off my head on something.

Now I had been to rehab – even though it had done nothing for me – it was time for a follow-up piece. And so in June, just weeks after leaving the Nightingale, my agent called the paper and arranged for me to do another interview. In this one, which was accompanied by photographs of me playing tennis, to prove I was '100% fit', I talked about how I had successfully overcome my battle with cocaine addiction and vowed never to touch the stuff again. 'Cocaine ruined my life,' I told the paper. 'I'd look in the mirror and see this horrible gaunt face. I hardly recognised myself.' It was, of course, just one big lie. Not only was I still using the drug, but I remember taking it just minutes before I did the interview.

8

BACK TO ALBERT SQUARE

....

By the time I checked out of the Nightingale in 1995 I certainly didn't possess any of the attributes that I would need to get to the top of my career. I had told the *Mirror* interviewer in June how I was looking forward to getting back to work and referred to all the offers I had been made. It was all fanciful talk, of course. The reality was that I had got so bad that I could no longer really function properly, let alone hold down a job. There had been a time in my life, during my teens, when I wouldn't have let anything come between me and my ambition, not even a relationship. What was now so pathetic and tragic was that by the age of twenty-one I'd reached the point where I wouldn't and couldn't let anything come between me and my addiction to cocaine.

After I left *EastEnders* I had spoken in interviews about how I wanted to make a career for myself in film and would even consider going to Hollywood if the right opportunity came my way. There was no question that this was my ambition at the time. I really wanted to make it as an actress, and if I wasn't going to be the next Jodie Foster then I would carve a name for myself as a respected television actress in this country instead. I had so many plans for the future, so many dreams, and I really believed that I could achieve them if I put my mind to it. But it is, of course, very hard to put your mind to anything when you have addiction issues. You simply don't have the focus, the energy, the desire or the will.

I had also lost the hunger to work. I'd go for weeks without even thinking about it. But it didn't bother me. I had worked since the age of seven and was quite enjoying having some time off, if I'm honest about it. After the Nightingale I went back to my old ways and carried on killing time, going out and taking drugs for the rest of that year.

But as I continued down this route it was beginning to dawn on me just how much money I was getting through. I realised that I couldn't survive on my savings for ever, especially when I was living that kind of lifestyle, and as I wasn't on television I was no longer getting as many offers for modelling work either. I was going to have to get back out there.

So the call from the producers at *EastEnders* in 1996 couldn't have come at a more opportune moment for me. The soap was suffering from poor ratings and so they decided, as they normally do when that happens, to bring some familiar faces back on to the Square. The producers were aware of my addiction by now. They had read all about it in the papers, but they had also read that I was now clean. They called me in for a brief meeting and the subject was touched on gently, but once I assured them that I was well, ready to work again, and had put all that behind me, they invited me back for another year.

It felt good to be back in the fold again. I liked the idea of being part of the show once more, earning regular money, having a routine and seeing my old friends. Maybe this was just what I needed, I thought. Maybe if I went back I could focus on work again and get some normality back into my life. My mother was pleased. She thought this was just what I needed. If I was on set every day working, back doing the job I loved, then perhaps I might see the light. Perhaps I just needed some structure, a bit of discipline, to put me back on the straight and narrow.

Walking on to the set on my first day back felt like coming home. Everyone was so warm and friendly, so nice to me, that any apprehensions I had about re-turning to the soap quickly disappeared. There had been a couple of cast changes since I left, but a lot of my old friends were still there. Ross and Steve were still in the show, as were Sid, Mike, June and Wendy. The only people I had yet to meet and get to know well in terms of my story-lines were Martine McCutcheon, who played Grant's love interest Tiffany, and Barbara

Windsor, my on-screen mother, who had recently been written into the story.

I loved Martine right from the word go. She was just the sweetest, most unaffected and grounded girl I had ever met in the industry. She always had a lovely disposition, always so cheerful and so sunny, no matter what was going on with her, and she was adored by everyone.

'Everything all right, Danni?' she'd say when we met on set or in make-up, her brown eyes twinkling like stars. 'Let's have a natter and a cup of tea in my dressing-room later on.'

Before I went back to the soap I had been extremely nervous about how I was going to get on with Barbara Windsor, who had been cast as the Mitchell children's mother Peggy. Barbara had always been one of my biggest idols. As a child I had loved her in the *Carry On* movies and I couldn't really get over the fact that I was not only going to be on set with her but that we would be working so closely together. But any doubts I had about how we would get on were dispelled as soon as we met. She instantly took me under her wing and looked after me as though I really was her daughter. Every morning when I got on set she would knock on my dressing-room door to see how I was and we would spend hours together talking about everything from our story-lines within the soap to our own personal plot-lines outside of it.

We quickly formed a close friendship and every day

we would go and get some lunch from the canteen and take it back to her dressing-room, where we would sit and go over our lines together. I was lucky with my story-lines, because they had me working with some of my closest friends, whether it was Ross or Sid or Martine. My favourite day on set was Friday, when we would film in the Vic. At that time Sam, Peggy and Frank were all working in the bar together, so whether we had any lines or not Mike, Barbara and I would have to be there in the background pulling pints and clearing the empties all day long. The three of us would stand there all day gossiping to one another. Mike, an avid golf fan, would bring his putter and a ball into work and if he wasn't putting would practise his drive behind the bar, in between takes. If someone was fluffing up their lines or taking too long over a scene he'd joke: 'Come on, get it together. I could be on the golf course, you know!'

For a while being back on set was just pure magic and I enjoyed every day of it. I was keen to make a good impression with everyone there, and so to start with I kept my working life and my private life separate. I would only use the drug when I wasn't working, and for the first few weeks was conscientious about not going out late at night and arriving at work on time, with all my lines learnt.

But it didn't last long. Within a month of me being at work, getting into the swing of things again and of receiving my first wage packet I was back to my old ways. I was out and about at night again doing the scene. I was using as much as ever, going out till dawn, as often as I possibly could. I thought for a while that I was getting away with it. I thought I was holding together and that, despite all the press that had surrounded my drug addiction the year before, I had managed to convince all my co-workers that I had put it behind me. What I didn't realise is that they were, in fact, all too painfully aware that I was still coming to terms with my demons and were doing everything they possibly could to protect and look after me.

When I returned to the soap June, Mike and Wendy, for example, requested that I should have my dressing-room down their end of the corridor, away from the younger cast members, just so they could keep an eye on me. Throughout the day they would pop into my room to make sure I was OK, and they would spend their free time with me because they could see I was still very vulnerable. I was so thin by then that they were always trying to feed me up, and there wasn't a day when one of them wasn't asking me to lunch or tea.

June and Wendy had tried to talk to me about my problems and to encourage me to confide in them, but I just didn't want to have the conversation with any of them. I wasn't ready for it. I was in such a state of denial myself that I was hardly going to sit down and admit I had a problem to anyone else. Barbara and I spent a lot of time together and could talk about anything, but when it came to drugs she knew that I wasn't going to open up to her. It was a difficult line for her to tread. Because of our on-screen relationship she didn't want to damage our off-screen one; she knew I was vulnerable and didn't want to upset me. She wanted to be there for me, not have me running off in the opposite direction.

With Mike it was different. He was always direct with me and said exactly what was on his mind. He had been in the industry a long time and had seen a lot of friends ruin their lives and careers through addictions to alcohol and drugs, and he didn't want to see that happen to me.

'Look, princess,' he'd say to me, 'you've got to stop messing with that stuff. You're ruining your life, you're running your pretty little face. You used to be a little breath of fresh air, you used to have these dancing eyes, this sparkle about you – now look at you. You look so ill. It's not good for you, you have to stop. I've seen that shit kill people, princess. It's poison, you mustn't touch the stuff.'

But like the little fool I was I didn't listen to Mike. I thought I was on top of it. I didn't really think that it was his or anyone else's business for that matter. But of course it was. Looking back I can't really believe how incredibly selfish I was. So long as I carried on using drugs and working with these people it *was* their business and it affected them all.

Fortunately my co-workers were all consummate professionals, unlike me, and they carried me through it for as long as they could. Whether it was the sweet girls in make-up who didn't bat an eyelid when I nodded off in morning sessions with them, the directors and cameramen who patiently stood by as I did take after take, or the actors who learnt how to cope when I fluffed my lines and found they were having to prompt me through scenes – they all supported me.

During the time that I had been off work I had been taking the drug during the day. I would use it to give me a boost when I needed it. Now that I was working five or six days a week and juggling that with my social life as well, I found that I needed that kick-start more than ever. And so, within a couple of months of returning to work and burning the candle at both ends, I started to use cocaine at work, just so I could get through the day. I was so exhausted the whole time, I thought it was the only way forward. It started with just the odd little line here and there in the morning when I hadn't had much, or sometimes any sleep the night before. I used it as a little pick-me-up, in the way that anyone else might have a cappuccino before they started their work in the morning. But one or two lines were never enough and it didn't take long before I was using throughout the day. I'd come to shoot a scene and find myself having a little line just before I was called on set. Sometimes I'd have just enough time to have another, and so it went on. When I watch re-runs of those scenes now I can't believe how out of it I look. Cocaine may have kept me physically awake but it didn't make me feel any more alert, and rather than help me through the day my drug taking was just making me feel increasingly ill.

Sometimes I felt so bad that I just didn't know what to do. When I felt like that I'd go and knock on Martine's dressing-room door. Even though she was quite a bit younger than I was there was something so maternal about Martine's friendship with me. She was always so caring and sweet to me and even though I had brought all my problems on myself, she never once judged me and never turned me away. Instead she'd open her door to me, no matter what she was up to, and let me be with her until I felt better. However bad I was she would greet me with her beautiful, cheery face.

'What's up, Danni?' she'd say when I came knocking.

'I don't know, Martine. I'm just not feeling so good today.'

And with that she'd invite me in.

'What you need is a nice big cup of tea and a little lie down.'

And before I knew it she'd put the kettle on and was making me up a bed on her sofa. I'd lie there all afternoon, curled up like a foetus, covered in blankets, which she would rearrange as I lay there, plumping up pillows and cushions, and she'd just do her thing and chat away to me. Sometimes, if I was lucky, she'd sing me songs. It was like my own personal lullaby. 'You OK, Danni darling?' she'd say to me from time to time. She became my lifeline.

Martine didn't have to be nice to me. She was very popular on set and was friends with a lot of people in the cast who didn't have any time for me. If I am honest about it there was a bunch of new young cast members who, rightly or wrongly, didn't like me. I remember doing a scene one day in the Vic and one of them just stood there laughing at me, throwing pea-nuts in my direction every time I tried to deliver my lines. I probably deserved it, as far as they were concerned, but it didn't help anyone that day, not least the director, who kept having to re-shoot as the nuts flew. When Martine was invited to lunch with them and they didn't want me to come with her she would always come to my room and tell me that she wouldn't be long. 'I'll be back shortly, Danni,' she'd say. 'Will you be OK?' I'd tell her that I was fine and to go and have fun, and more often than not would end up in Barbara's room having lunch with her instead.

By now my drug taking was having a serious effect on my work. I was often late into the studio in the morning. In that world being on time for work was everything, because if you were late just by half an hour – even for a costume fitting or make-up – you were not only in danger of holding up shooting but you could mess up a whole day's filming schedule, costing the producers thousands of pounds. I was hauled up in front of the producers on several occasions about my time-keeping, but I didn't pay too much attention. I would apologise, of course, and say that I wouldn't do it again, only to be late again the following week.

Most people in that situation, knowing the importance of being at work on time, would go home to bed at a reasonable hour, set their alarm clock, have a good night's sleep and be up fresh as a daisy the following morning. But not me, oh no – that was far too much to expect from me by then. To get to bed at decent hour – let's say even at midnight, which is late by most people's standards – would have meant leaving the West End or South London sometime after eleven, which was usually when my evening started to get going. But I wasn't going to let a little thing like punctuality get in the way of my life, and so I found a way round it.

My little ruse was not to go home to bed but to drive straight to work when I came out of a club or spill at five or six in the morning. I'd go to my dressing-room and get a couple of hours of shut-eye in there before work began. After a couple of weeks of doing this, night after night, the security guards at Elstree got wise to me and mentioned it to the show's producers, who were not happy. They called me in to have a chat and told me that my behaviour simply wasn't acceptable. There was no mention of drugs, nothing about me

taking cocaine; they just made rather oblique refer-
ences to my party lifestyle. I never slept in my dressing-
room again after that lecture, but I didn't start going
home to bed to sleep either. Instead, after a night out,
I'd get into my car, crawl on to the back seat and go to
sleep under my coat until it was time to go to work.

This hard living was finally beginning to take its toll
on my body. Even if I managed to catch a couple of
hours' sleep in the car it still wasn't enough to survive
on. I was always tired, and I couldn't think straight.
Half the time my head was foggy, and I'd have to take
numerous naps throughout the day. I'd force myself to
eat chocolate so as to get some glucose into my system
and raise my energy levels. I'd drink copious amounts
of coffee in order to stay awake. By now I was only
eating one meal a day. Come lunchtime I'd go to the
BBC canteen and force a large plate of egg and chips,
hardly the most nutritious choice on the menu, down
me, simply for sustenance. I couldn't eat first thing in
the morning because I was too tired, felt too ill or just
couldn't face it, and I never ate in the evening because
by then I had been taking coke all day and it's a
powerful appetite suppressant.

Somehow I managed to get through the day, but
because I wasn't firing on all cylinders it was hardly
my best work and often I would have a problem
concentrating on my scenes. I was having problems
learning my lines and trying to remember what was
going on in scenes I was shooting. A lot of the time the

other cast members would try to cover for me, but there were moments when they simply couldn't carry it off.

When I drove home from work in the evening on the M25 I would do so with the heating turned down and the car windows wide open, whatever the weather, just to keep myself from falling asleep at the wheel. Sometimes I was just so exhausted that I'd have to pull over and take a nap on the hard shoulder. No matter how much gear I was doing I just couldn't stay awake. I had no energy in me, no nutrients, nothing to burn except my own body fat. My brain may have felt awake but my body was knackered. It simply couldn't take it any more.

One afternoon, about six months into my second stint on the show, I was filming a scene that involved Martine and Ross on the set of the Queen Vic. I actually have no recollection of that day, and I only know about it because Ross told me afterwards what happened. All I know is that I was supposed to be having a conversation with Ross. I was standing on the staircase at the back of the pub, while he was at the bottom of it. According to him the scene went as planned and I managed to deliver my lines perfectly, but as soon as the director yelled cut I passed out, falling like timber and collapsed on top of him. Had it been anyone less strong and well built I probably would have knocked them to the ground, but luckily for me it was Ross and he caught me in his arms.

The director and the producer were screaming at me. 'Get up and work!' 'Ross, get her up, make her work!'

And he just turned round and said, very calmly but firmly, 'No. No, I won't! Can't you see she's ill?' And with that he picked me up and carried me in his arms to the costume department, laid me down and called a doctor. I don't know what the doctor did, all I know was that when I was well enough I was sent home in cab.

Ross was terribly kind to me about it, as was Martine, who told the director I was just 'poorly'. They both knew that I was really ill by now and Ross was very worried about me. He knew that I hadn't been eating and that I wasn't sleeping properly. But there was nothing he could do. He knew I wouldn't listen, that I was beyond his help. He cared about me, as they all did, but short of living some one else's life twenty-four hours a day what can you do? All he could say to me was: 'You're trusting all the wrong people, Danniella.'

Quite amazingly I was never reprimanded for what happened that day. No one said anything to me. It was never mentioned again, but clearly the producers now had serious doubts about my future on the soap. I was proving to be a liability. My behaviour was interfering with the schedule. It was interfering with the other cast members' work. There were days when I just didn't bother showing up for work at all. The dilemma they faced was what to do with me. They had only just written my character back into the soap; now, within months, they were having to write her out of it all over again. They felt bad about getting rid of me, too. I could tell that they felt responsible for me but of course ultimately there wasn't very much they could do to help – and I wasn't their problem.

Within a couple of weeks I was called into a meeting and told very politely that were going to let me go early and terminate my contract. They would, they explained, gradually write my character out of the script again, which would take a couple of months to do.

I can't remember how I felt really at that precise moment. I was probably a little numb, but I knew deep down that I had brought it on myself and had given them no choice. When June found out she was distraught. She went straight to the second floor where the producers' offices were and begged them to give me a second chance. 'She's not a bad kid, she's just not well. Getting rid of her isn't going to help her, it might just make things worse. Please let her stay. She's a good little actress.' But the producers just couldn't. They just couldn't afford the time or the money that was keeping me there.

June came to me and gave me a hug. 'I'm really going to miss you, Danniella. I want you to take care of yourself and come back.' June had been on the show when I first joined the soap. She had watched me grow up. She couldn't bear what was happening to me. I was sad to be leaving her, too. She and I had become close over the years and I had been so proud to work with her. My other friends on the set – especially Ross, Mike, Barbara and of course Martine – were sad to see me go too, but I believe they thought it was the best thing for me. They wanted me to go and get myself better, that I was too vulnerable and sick to be working in that kind of environment.

The producers were very nice about it all. Rather than killing my character off they sent her to Spain, once again leaving the door open for her to return. Maybe they hoped that I might come to my senses one day and clean up my act. There was no official line as to why I was leaving, and when the announcement was made the following week they were kind enough to let me say in interviews that I was going because I wanted 'a change of direction'.

'Hopefully, one day I'll return to the show,' I told journalists, 'nothing is set in stone.'

'I'd like to come back one day,' I said, 'if they'll have me.'

'For now I just want to do my own thing.' It was just one line after another, in every sense.

Of course, when I was given my marching orders that afternoon, deep down I was sad to be going. I was also terrified about my future and was unsure of what I was going to do next. But when the time came for me to shoot my final scene a couple of months later, all those thoughts had evaporated because, you see, I did have something to look forward to. I was pregnant.

9

MOTHERHOOD

....

I fell pregnant in March 1996 and discovered the fact just days after I had been told that my contract with *EastEnders* was being terminated. I had been having an on-off relationship with the baby's father, who was one of my South London friends, for a couple of months, and although the relationship was off again by the time I discovered the news, I knew right from day one that I wanted to keep my baby, to have this child. I hadn't intended to get pregnant, that was the last thing on my mind, but it was just one of those things. In many ways it was astonishing that I was even fertile, given the abuse I had put my body through, but it had happened and there I was, at the age of twenty-two, eight months away from becoming a mother for the first time.

I didn't get a chance to tell my parents face to face, which I was sad about, because when I was younger I had often thought about the moment when I would tell them that they were about to become grandparents for the first time. Instead my mother learnt of my pregnancy from the front page of the *Sun*. The girl behind the counter at the chemist where I bought my pregnancy test must have rung the paper and sold the story before I'd even got home and had the chance to use it. Mum rang the next morning, really upset.

'Why didn't you have the decency to tell me?' she asked.

'I only found out myself last night!' I replied.

Dad didn't say much when I called him later to talk about it. He had given up on me by then.

Those who knew me had a range of different reactions when they heard the news. There were those who thought that this could be the best thing for me, that it would be the incentive that I needed to finally kick my habit once and for all. And there were others who questioned, quite justifiably, given that I couldn't look after my own life and be responsible for that, how on earth I was going to care for another person. Some people thought the baby might not live because I was so thin and unhealthy. Others assumed that I would have a termination because of my habit, my career and, I guess, my pure selfishness.

I knew what I wanted to do but I was still having to hear all these different opinions on a daily basis. No one, it seemed, would let me make my own mind up about it. No one thought I was capable of such a decision. It was Mike Read who finally came to my rescue. I was still working on the soap then and would soon be filming my final story-line, which would see my character leave Albert Square. Mike knew that I was being given a hard time by everyone around me, and he also knew that this was a decision that I would have to come to myself. I was due some time off from the soap, so Mike went out and bought me a ticket to Spain, where he and his wife owned a villa.

'You're going to stay at my house and have a break,' he said. 'Go and have a think. Take your time. I have a friend who will look after you when you are there, so you can just relax and spend time thinking about what you want to do. And whatever decision you come to I'll stand by you.'

It was one of the kindest and most thoughtful things anyone has ever done for me, and I was touched. Spain was the best place for me. I could escape from everyone and make my own mind up about what I wanted to do in peace. I could escape from people's opinions, escape from the press, and best of all I could escape from drugs. I had always found that getting away from my usual environment meant that I could leave the drugs behind, too. Holidays meant time off from coke, even if I started to use again as soon as I got home. After a blissful cocaine-free week I returned to London, reasonably healthy and happy and excited about the prospect of becoming a mother.

Once I told my mother my decision she and my father vowed to stand by me. They promised to do whatever they could to help me and the baby once it was born. My mother hoped that I would give up drugs now – at least while I was carrying the baby. However, it wasn't to be, and although this is one of the hardest, most shameful things to admit, I used cocaine throughout my pregnancy.

I didn't stop. I didn't even cut down. I used as much as I did before. I used every single day that child lay in my womb. I continued to party, I continued to smoke, I continued to drink and I still wasn't really eating properly. It was horrific, I was horrific. And though I am totally to blame for this, totally responsible for my actions, what also bothers me now looking back is that no one in my social circle tried to stop me. Not one of these so-called friends ever turned round to me, as I snorted yet another line, and asked me what the hell I thought I was doing. No one said a thing. People would take drugs with me, people would sell to me, people would give me Charlie for free. By this time I was no longer in regular contact with my ex-colleagues from *EastEnders* so the only people who tried to talk any sense into me were my parents and my doctor, who knew that I was still using. He explained the damage I could do to my child, but I am afraid that I just wouldn't listen to him.

Sometimes now, when I'm standing at the school gates at home time waiting to collect my beautiful little boy Kai, I look at the other mothers there and feel so dreadfully ashamed of the way I behaved. I look at them as they take their children by their hands and think I bet you didn't drink when you were having your baby, I bet you didn't smoke. I bet you looked after yourself, ate properly, slept, took vitamins and supplements so that you could give your baby the best start in life. But I did none of those things. I did nothing for my baby, as much as I wanted him and longed for him to come into my life. And on top of all that I took cocaine as well.

And then when my son runs towards me, smiling and laughing and clutching a picture he has done for me that day, looking like any other kid in the play-ground, I realise how blessed I am. How lucky I am that, despite everything I did, I have this healthy, happy little boy.

Kai was born on Saturday 23 November 1996 at London's Whipps Cross Hospital, a couple of weeks after my twenty-third birthday. He weighed in at 6lb 10 oz.

I didn't have an epidural for the birth. I didn't have time, I was only in labour for an hour and a half as it was, and in any case I didn't need the hospital's drugs – not when I had my own supply. I used cocaine throughout my labour, taking my final line just half an hour before I went to the hospital and as soon as they took him off to be cleaned and weighed I used the drug again. My parents were with me in the delivery room, and so I used the excuse of needing to go to the bathroom and while I was in there I took a line. I am not trying to sound callous or melodramatic about my drug use; I am just trying to tell it the way it was. I was so dependent on the drug I couldn't help myself.

I was pleased but not surprised when they told me I had given birth to a son. Even during the earliest stages of my pregnancy I was sure he would be a boy. I didn't have a test to see what he would be. I didn't have to, I just knew. When I spoke about my baby it was always 'he' not 'it', and when I dreamt about what my child would look like when he was born I always saw a baby boy.

I may have known that my baby was going to be a boy, but I didn't expect him to be healthy. I was racked with both fear and guilt at the prospect that he might be ill, be disabled in some way or die at birth because of my negligence. My obstetrician knew that I was using drugs when I was pregnant with Kai, and so when he was born and they took him away to be weighed they also ran a series of blood and urine tests on him to make sure that he was OK. The samples were then sent over to specialists at the Great Ormond Street children's hospital. To my eternal relief, his results were good. He was completely healthy and there was nothing in his system at all. He had tested negative for everything.

I am not the first drug addict to have a baby. Nor am I the first one to give birth to a healthy child either. But what I would like to stress is just how lucky I was. If you think of the damage that you can do to a foetus just by smoking or drinking, then just consider what I was putting my unborn child through. I was taking as much as five grams of coke a day, washing it down with a potent cocktail of alcohol and cigarette smoke. The fact that Kai had no cocaine in his blood system when he was born was, in fact, extraordinary. The medical staff at the hospital made it very clear that he was lucky to be alive. To me it felt like a miracle.

When the nurse placed my tiny baby in my arms for the first time, I looked at this angelic little thing, who was perfect in every way, and I said to him, 'You're a right little fighter, aren't you?' I couldn't really believe that I had been that lucky, that he was alive and that he was OK. I didn't deserve that, I didn't deserve him. And I vowed that from that moment onwards, whatever happened, nothing would come between us and that I would give him the best life I possibly could.

The problem was that I wasn't really fit to make my child those promises. The reality of the situation was that I was an out-of-work, single mother, who was addicted to drugs. If I was going to be a good mother then I should at least try to get on top of my addiction, but I still couldn't manage it. Mum had prayed that once I had Kai I might see the light and try to sort out my problems. I think she harboured the hope that once I had a baby to look after I would change, that now I had another life to care for I might try to do something about my own. But sadly, for her and for Kai, it didn't work like that and I continued to use.

In every other way I tried to do my best by Kai. His father and I even tried to get back together for his sake, but pretty early on we realised that our relationship was never going to work and it was, in the long run, going to do Kai more harm than good being surrounded by two people who could never stop fighting.

As far as my career was concerned I was happy to keep it on hold for the moment. I had nothing to rush back to anyway, now that I was out of *EastEnders* again, and all I really wanted to do was be with my baby. I was lucky in the fact that I didn't have to work. I had sold my flat in Buckhurst Hill and we had moved to a rented house for the moment. And thanks to my mother I still had my savings so we had enough to live on. But Mum was no fool. She knew that if she gave me access to all my money I would just end up spending it all on drugs, so she gave me an allowance from my investments, which was just enough for Kai and me to be comfortable.

However, without enough money for me to feed my addiction, I was anything but. I didn't just *want* drugs anymore, I felt that I needed them. In the way that my baby needed his milk to survive, I believed I needed cocaine. But I didn't have enough money to feed my baby and my habit. If I was to buy the amount of cocaine I was used to taking, I'd need to spend just over £1,200 a week on the drug.

In the old days I would have done a few modelling shoots to get round this problem, but now that I was out of the soap it was difficult for me to get the kind of fees I had once commanded. Nevertheless, I put myself out there and did as many as I could. I'd do magazine interviews too. The celebrity press would pay quite a decent amount of money for an interview, particularly if it was a mother and baby shoot. And so I'd 'invite them into my home', as they say in that world, and pose for their photographers in a variety of different outfits with my baby in my arms. And in the interviews I would talk about the 'joys of motherhood', my 'hopes for the future' and how great it felt 'to finally be free from drugs'.

I *was* overjoyed to be a mother and I *did* have hopes for the future, but I certainly wasn't free from drugs. It was all such a lie, but it was one that I had got used to living and the press seemed happy to swallow it, for the time being at least.

10

ADDICT

....

I think a lot of people were surprised by how easily I took to motherhood. Many of them had probably assumed that within weeks of having Kai I would get bored and dump him with my mother or a child-minder and go off partying. But it wasn't like that. From the moment Kai came into my life I fell completely in love with him. He was my focus, my reason to live, and like many new mothers I couldn't think how I had ever lived without him. I felt so complete, so fulfilled. It didn't matter if I wasn't working: that world, that life seemed so empty by comparison. For now, all I wanted was to be with my son.

And this is how it was for the first couple of years. Kai never left my side, as I was always loath to leave him with other people, even if I was just popping out for an hour or two. I was determined that he should have a happy and a normal childhood. I followed a routine with him, feeding, bathing and putting him to bed at regular times. I made sure he always looked nice and had good clothes. And as he grew from a tiny baby to a little toddler I spent time reading to him and playing with him.

I always wanted the best for Kai and gave him as much love and attention as I could but I was aware that as a single mother I couldn't give him as much as two parents could. I was desperate to give him a stable home, and so in a rash move in October 1998 I got married. I hadn't known the man in question for very long. He was a dispatch rider and I had met him by chance whilst filling up my car at a service station. Within days we had met up for a date, within weeks we were an item, and then suddenly we had decided to spend the rest of our lives together. I can see now just how impulsive it all was, but at the time it felt right. I guess I was vulnerable and lonely, but it was a mistake and we soon realised we had little in common. Within the space of eight months I was filing for divorce.

I realised then that I couldn't get involved with people just for Kai's sake. A relationship was only ever going to work if I really wanted it. For now it was going to have to be just me and Kai, our little team, and I vowed to give him as much love as two parents would.

I loved Kai from the word go, but I can't pretend that he had an idyllic childhood in those early years. He couldn't have, because I was still using drugs. I no longer went out at night, I didn't want to, I wanted to be at home with him, but that didn't stop me from using. I was still taking just as many drugs as before. I couldn't stop myself. My addiction had now reached the point where it had become an actual physical sickness and by that I mean I felt ill without them. It was no longer a case of using coke to get a kick or have a good time. Without it I felt shaky, nervous and lacking in energy. I believed that I needed it to survive, and so throughout the day and night I would take coke in the way other people eat and drink to stay alive. I couldn't function without it, or so I thought.

I imagined, as most addicts do before they finally admit to their problem, that I had my habit under control. I was, after all, managing my life, looking after my child and was able to stick to his routine. I was never completely out of it. I was never reeling drunk or so high that I didn't know what I was doing, where or who I was. But I was doing drugs whenever I could, and that wasn't good for either of us.

During the first two years of Kai's life I didn't see many people except for a couple of friends who also used, my dealers and my family. When Kai was born I made my peace with my mother and father for his sake and we kept in regular contact. They had always been very unhappy about my use of drugs, and now that I had a child this was all the more alarming to them, but there was very little they could do about it. Every time they confronted me about it I would fly off the handle, and after a while they stopped doing so because they were frightened that if things became too heated between us I would break off contact with them once again, and they didn't think that would be good for Kai's welfare. They knew they had to be there for me and just accept the situation for what it was. They knew that I was trying to be a good mother and that, despite my drug addiction, I was somehow managing to cope. And so for the first fifteen months of Kai's life this is how things were, and everything seemed to go quite smoothly until February 1998, when I was involved in a horrific car accident, which nearly cost me my life.

The accident had nothing to do with my drug taking. It was a straightforward car crash. I was in the car with Kai when someone drove into us from the side at a set of traffic lights. It was entirely their fault. The impact of the crash was so severe that when the car hit us, crashing into my side of the car, I was thrown out of the windscreen on to the bonnet and then fell to the road. Kai was fine because he was in his baby seat in the back but I was so badly hurt that I flat-lined twice on the way to the hospital. My eye had come away from its socket and I had to have over 40 stitches in my face. For a while it was touch and go, but after the first 24 hours the doctors thought I would pull through, although they weren't convinced that I would look the same again. When my parents saw me they were horrified. The tissue round my eye, which by this time had been put back into place, was severely swollen, so much so that I could barely open it and blinking was painful. My complexion was a deep purple as my face was badly bruised, and covered with scratches and cuts where the glass had been embedded in my skin. My nose was flattened, as though I had done ten rounds in a boxing ring. I was a mess.

Whilst I lay in hospital Mum took care of Kai and my family came to see me as often as possible. It took weeks before I recovered and I was in a lot of pain, but I got through it and, unbelievably, once the bruising had gone down and the stitches were removed, I was as good as new. My family and the doctors were amazed. They had all thought I would be disfigured, but I didn't have a single scar on my face. I looked just the same as ever but that wasn't to last, for within the space of a year my nose collapsed, and it had, I will finally now admit, nothing to do with the crash.

In January 1999 I was lying in my bed one night trying, for once, to get some sleep. Like most people who do a lot of cocaine I was sniffing away, trying to clear my airways, which were permanently blocked, when I felt this strange sensation in my nose. It felt and sounded like a faint crackle. I got up and went to the bathroom to look in the mirror and gasped when I saw my reflection. The wall of cartilage and skin that separated my nostrils was badly damaged. It hadn't fallen out, it was still there, but it had split completely. It didn't hurt me – it wouldn't have done, there was so much coke up there I wouldn't have felt a thing – and there was no blood either. There couldn't have been because, as I was to learn, all the blood cells were dead. All I felt was a numbness. Physical numbness and, I suppose, an emotional one as well.

Rather than ring a doctor or make my way to a casualty department as a normal person would have done in that situation, I just stood there frozen, staring at my image in the mirror, wondering what to do. It was too late at night to call my mother and ask for help, and I was too high to go to a hospital, and so not knowing what I should do next I went back to bed and hid under the covers. I think I hoped that if I got some sleep I might wake up in the morning and find that it had all been just a very bad dream.

Sadly, that was not the case. When I looked in the mirror the following morning the split was still there, and in the light of day it looked worse. When I put my head back and looked up into my nose I could see the extent of the damage. There was very little left of the cartilage that divided one nostril from the other. This wasn't just a superficial wound. I hadn't just split my septum. It was far worse than that. A whole part of the inside of my nose had actually come away and was just hanging there.

I grabbed the phone and rang my mother.

'My nose has gone,' I said.

'What do you mean your nose has gone?' she asked.

'It's gone. My nose has gone. My nose has gone!'

There was a pause. I don't think she understood

what I was saying. 'You'd better come straight over,' she said.

I got Kai up, dressed him and gave him his breakfast, all the time trying to keep my head down so that he couldn't see up my nose. He was only two years old and I didn't want him to be frightened by my appearance. When he was ready I bundled him into the car and drove to Mum's place.

When I arrived at her house and lifted my head up slightly to show her, I thought she was going to faint. She clasped her hand over her mouth and went very pale, as though all the blood in her body had just drained out of her. She looked for a moment as though she was about to throw up. She steadied herself on the arm of a chair and got her breath back.

'Right, we're going to the hospital, now. I'm taking you to casualty,' she said once she had calmed down. She started looking around the room for her bags and keys.

'No way!' I said, panicking. 'No way!' I was now shouting. 'There's no way you're taking me to hospital. I'm not going, no way. It'll be all over the papers tomorrow if I go there.'

And with that I got Kai and left.

I suppose that for most people in my situation this would have been the moment when they got the wake-up call they needed. The moment they would have stopped using. But not me, no. It wasn't enough for me that I had destroyed my looks and that I now had a deformed nose, all thanks to my cocaine addiction. Rather than vow never to touch the stuff again – what did I do? I went out and scored some more, because that was the only way I knew of dealing with the situation, of dealing with anything for that matter. Getting high and out of it was the only way I could cope.

The damage I had done to my nose hadn't just happened overnight but through years of cocaine abuse. That fine white powder I had put up my nose day after day, year after year, had corroded the tissue and cartilage that separated my nostrils, wearing it down bit by bit, day by day, until there was nothing left. I have since learnt that it is actually quite a common occurrence in people who take coke on a regular basis. A doctor I consulted told me that as many as one in eight people who use cocaine a lot can suffer from holes in their colonna wall.

In my case it probably started as a tiny hole, so small that I wouldn't have noticed it was there, but as I took more of the drug that hole would have become bigger and bigger until it eventually split. I guess I didn't see the signs because I was always too out of it, and by that stage wasn't paying too much attention to my appearance. But in the months that led up to this what had happened was that the cells in my nose had slowly begun to die because there was no blood supply there. And even back then, though I didn't take much notice of it at the time, if the sun was shining and you looked at me in profile you could almost see straight through my nose: the skin was so thin and transparent it was like tracing paper.

I ignored my mother's pleas to see a doctor or consult a specialist and carried on using every day for the next month. This of course just made it worse, until it got to the stage when all that was left of my colonna was a tiny little blob at the front of my nose. A section of the cartilage within my nose had completely disintegrated, and every time I wiped or blew it, more would come away.

My mother was distraught about what I had done to myself and was determined that something should be done about my nose, whatever my feelings were about it. She wanted me to see someone who could perhaps rebuild it if I was lucky or, at the very least, stop it from getting any worse. And so she started on her mission, consulting a long list of surgeons who specialised in rhinoplasty. There are, of course, thousands of surgeons in this country who are qualified to re-shape a nose: iron down the unsightly bump you have been a little self-conscious of, take in your flared nostrils, make the tip of your nose a little more pert and sexy. Reconstructing a nose from scratch, on the other hand, rebuilding the interior and creating a divide so that a person looks relatively normal – that's a tall order. But my mother, true to form, was persistent in her search and eventually she struck gold.

Mr James Frame was a Harley Street plastic surgeon who worked at the Springfields Hospital, in Chelmsford. He was renowned in his field for reconstructive work. He had been highly recommended to my mother and, after a great deal of arm-twisting and assurances that he would treat my case confidentially, I agreed to go with her to see him.

Mr Frame couldn't quite believe what he saw when I sat before him in his consultation room at the hospital. As he examined me, and took measurements of my nose or what was left of it, he was polite enough not to say anything, but I could see that he was shocked. He told me later that he had never in his whole career seen a case like it. He had treated patients with similar problems but none quite as bad as mine.

After he had finished the examination he went back to his desk, sat down and made a couple of notes and then put down his pen and looked me in eye. He told me that he could help me, that he could reconstruct my nose, and would be happy to do so, but explained in no uncertain terms that if I carried on taking cocaine after that, not only would my nose collapse again, but the next time it could be a lot worse. He explained that if that happened there was a strong possibility that my nose could never be fixed again. He asked me if I understood the implications of what he was saying. I nodded.

He then came over to me again and looked at my nose in profile and then looked at my mother's, who

ADDICT

was sitting next to me. 'Don't give me a nose like hers, for God's sake!' I said. To this day I'm not sure why I said it. My mother has a very pretty nose, but I guess it was just indicative of how I was at the time, always lashing out at others, even when they were doing everything they could to help me.

Mr Frame arranged, much to my mother's delight and relief, to carry out the operation the very next morning. However, it did not go to plan. Despite the fact that I wasn't supposed to eat or drink anything after midnight the night before my operation, I thought nothing about having a couple of lines of cocaine. When they came to take my blood the next morning it was so full of the stuff that the operation had to be postponed because it was deemed too dangerous to put me under the anaesthetic whilst I had coke in my system. And so they had to wait until later in the day before they could start the surgery.

The operation itself was a huge success. Mr Frame had managed, somehow, to reconstruct the inside of my nose, and unless you looked really carefully you would never have known that anything had happened to it. It was near perfect.

But just two weeks later the colonna collapsed again and I was back to where I started. It was nothing to do with Mr Frame's work. Had I heeded his advice my nose would look now as it did when I was a teenager. But I didn't. Like the fool I was I carried on using. I never gave myself a break. I didn't even give my nose a chance to heal after the operation. In fact as soon as they removed the wadding from my newly constructed nostrils after the operation and said that I was fit enough to go home, I rang my dealer and arranged for him to call round at my home later that day.

I was too embarrassed to return to Mr Frame after that. My mother was too upset with me to insist that I should. And so my nose stayed like that until 2001, when, clean at last, I finally felt both the need and the desire to have it fixed again.

Now as a born and bred Loughton girl my looks had always been important to me. Even as a young teenager I was always concerned about how I looked. It wasn't really a question of being vain, although I admit that, like most other girls, I had my moments. It was more about always looking nice and being well turned out. Where I came from women took care of their appearance. They wore nice clothes and paid attention to their hair and make-up. You'd never catch a woman from Loughton in some scruffy tracksuit, with unbrushed hair and dirty nails, even if she was just walking the dog. Going to the beauty salon or hairdressers was not an indulgence or a special treat, it was what people from Loughton did on a regular, perhaps even weekly, basis. It was a showy area and you had to look your best – and that's how I was brought up. And because I worked in showbusiness from an early age I was probably more conscious of all this than most people. Even as a young child I liked to look my best. I enjoyed wearing nice clothes, having my hair done by my mother and getting dressed up for parties.

So I might have been expected to be devastated by the loss of my nose. But in truth I wasn't really. I didn't really care. And, to be completely honest about it, there were moments, albeit when I was totally off my head, when I saw the benefits of losing my colonna. Now, you see, I could get even more coke up my nose when I took a line and, as degrading as that might sound, that was how my mind worked. I had lost, through my addiction, all sense of pride, all sense of respect and self-worth. I no longer cared about how I looked, I just cared about being high.

In terms of my physical appearance it wasn't just my nose that was affected by my cocaine abuse. As I took more and more of the drug it began to take its toll on the rest of my body.

Cocaine is a well-known appetite suppressant, which is one of the reasons why it has always been the drug of choice in the fashion industry. But anyone who thinks that surviving on a diet of champagne and cocaine will make you look like a supermodel should, believe me, think again. Coke did make me thin, there is no question about that. At the height of my addiction I weighed just six and a half stone, and even though I am only five foot four, it was by no means attractive. If you compare that, for example, with what I weigh today which is closer to nine stone, and consider that I am a size eight to ten now, that will give you an idea of just how scarily thin I was. If I stood naked you could count every bone in my rib-cage and spine. My hips protruded, my arms were scrawny, and my thighs were no bigger than the top of my arms are now. Any girl thinking that is a good look, or a good reason to take the drug, should read on.

Because I was eating, at the very most, one meal a day, there were no nutrients in my system whatsoever. Instead I survived on a diet of cocaine, alcohol and sugar – which came in the form of booze, caffeine and the odd bar of chocolate – all of which, as we know, are poisons to the body. The food I did manage to get down me was the for the most part pure junk, and I ate it only because I had to. I had no vegetables, fruit or protein in my diet, so I had no natural intake of vitamins and I certainly didn't think to take them in supplement form.

As a result I looked awful. Because I was so thin my cheeks and eye sockets were hollow. It got so bad at one point that I was known as 'Skeletor'. No one ever said: 'Gosh, Danni, you look great, you've lost so much weight.' They said: 'You look like a bloody skeleton.' And they were right. I did.

As a teenager I was lucky in that I always had good skin and very rarely got a spot. I had a natural glow about me, what they call a 'peaches and cream' complexion, and even when I was filming or model-ling I only ever had to wear the sheerest of founda-tions or powders. But by my early twenties my skin was grey and dull and I was prone to breakouts. When I was still taking care of myself I primed it twice a day with the most expensive moisturisers, cleansers and toners on the market, but by this time I had reached the stage where it was an effort even to wash my face. And when I did so, it was with a bar of cheap supermarket soap.

My hair, which had always been my great pride, was in a terrible state. It was lack-lustre, broke easily and felt like straw. I was born a natural blonde but as I got older it darkened a bit, so I would have my hair regularly highlighted at the hairdressers from the age of sixteen. If I saw the slightest hint of a root I'd rush to the salon to have it seen to. But during this period, when my addiction was bad, I never went. For two years I went without having my hair coloured and let it go mouse. I no longer cared; my self-regard was that low. But it wasn't just a case of not being bothered to go to the hairdresser, I could no longer afford to go to the London salons I once went to. If and when I did have that kind of money I preferred to spend it on drugs.

My eyes, once so blue and sparkly, looked dead. The whites were now yellow and bloodshot, and I had dark circles under them. My nails broke and didn't grow. There had been a time when I didn't go a week without having a manicure, but now they were ridged through lack of nutrition and torn and broken down to the quick.

When I looked in the mirror and saw my reflection, saw what I had become, I convinced myself that the mirror must be lying. I couldn't accept that this was how I really looked. I would go round my house from mirror to mirror checking my appearance. I'd go to the bathroom, decide that the light was all wrong. I'd try the one in my bedroom and think it was just as unflattering. I'd go to the sitting-room, dim the lights and take out a compact. But after a while, when I still couldn't get the reflection I wanted to see, I just gave up.

The main reason that the extent of the damage to my nose didn't come out sooner is that during the first six months after my nose collapsed I wasn't working. I couldn't really work. Being in the grip of the addiction I was essentially unemployable, but very occasionally, when I needed money, I would go and do the odd photographic shoot – but I would always insist that I worked with the same photographer.

Her name was Jeany Savage, and I had known her since I was a child and considered her to be a close friend. I had done my first advertising campaign with Jeany when I was starting out and had worked with her a lot over the years, so I knew I could trust her implicitly. I remember going to her studio for the first time after my nose went and she did a double take. She couldn't get over how I looked. It wasn't just the state of my nose that shocked her, although she was horrified by that – it was my whole appearance. There I was, this scraggy, thin, grey girl, with broken nails and hair like straw. It was as though a stranger had turned up for work that day.

'God, Danni,' she said when she saw me. 'Look at the state of you!'

She wasn't being mean, she was concerned about me, really concerned.

Gone was the bubbly, blonde, curvy girl with the sparkling eyes and the cheeky grin she was so used to working with. In her place was this lifeless shadow, a corpse-like creature with no spirit or soul.

Jeany was well aware that I was taking drugs and that I was addicted to them. And although she disapproved she knew that I really must need the money if I was going to come out to work looking like that. And she was right, my habit was costing me a lot – not just my looks but, of course, financially too. I was spending a lot on drugs and overheads such as rent, and I hadn't worked properly since I got pregnant. If I carried on like this I would have nothing left. And so, like the friend she was, Jeany waved her magic wand over me and performed every trick in her book to make me look good. She would spend hours making sure that I was lit well. She would shoot from the right angles and would always make sure when I posed that my head was slightly tilted downwards so that the camera never captured my missing colonna.

After the shoot she would spend hours retouching the photos. She would alter the hues of a photograph to make me look healthy and glowing, airbrushing out the bags and circles underneath my eyes, softening the hollows of my cheeks. Jeany was used to doing a little retouching after a shoot. With most girls she would use the airbrush to take in their thighs or flatten their tummies, but with me she was doing the reverse. She would work on a single photo for hours, trying to pad me out a bit, make me chunkier. She'd build up my face, add inches to my legs and arms and shade in my torso so you couldn't see my ribs underneath my clothes. In some shoots she'd put me in outsized jackets to hide my body, push-up bras to give me a chest, and hats that would be angled in such a way that you couldn't see my nose. We worked together with a wonderful make-up artist called Gary Cockerel who would cover me in foundation, highlighters, blushers and bronzers in an attempt to make me look half-way human.

Now that I had Kai I wasn't going out the way I used to, spending time at bars in the West End, and I no longer went clubbing, so I didn't have a problem with my appearance on that front. I surrounded myself with a very select and tight-knit group of friends – as unsavoury as they were – and other than that the only people I had regular contact with were my family. When I did have to venture out to go to the shops or take Kai for a walk I kept my head down. I perfected a new way of looking at people, which I still do to this day, because I was so conscious of them seeing the inside of my nose. I'd keep my head down, and bring my chin towards my neck and look up at them in the way that Princess Diana used to do when she was feeling a bit shy. And I certainly never threw my head back to laugh as I used to in the past. Because I am not the tallest person in the world it was all quite easy for me. In fact the only person who ever looked up at me and could see my nose was my son.

So for a time my secret was safe, but all that was to change in July 1999 when I was recalled to *EastEnders* for a third and final time. The recall was a mixed blessing. I was, of course, pleased that they wanted me back again after all that had happened and I looked forward to working once more, but because of my nose I dreaded going back as well. I couldn't cope with them finding out, I just didn't know how I was going to deal with it. I knew that within a minute of being in make-up my secret would be out. But I had no choice. I simply couldn't afford to turn the work down.

Like all resourceful addicts who become used to a life of denial and deception I found a way round the situation. Rather than come clean and say, 'Yes, my nose has collapsed as a result of my severe addiction to cocaine', I lied about it. Well, I didn't have much choice really. Once again my contract was only re-signed with the proviso that I was clean. Mal Young, the new producer of the show, hadn't worked with me before, so he didn't know what a handful I really was. He had been warned, and it had in fact even been suggested that they replace me with another actress, but he was loath to do so and he thought that it was only fair that I should be given another chance. I didn't want to blow it, so I decided that if anyone asked me about what had happened to my nose I would say that it had been damaged in the car crash. That was to be my excuse.

As it was, for the first couple of weeks, few people apart from the girls in make-up noticed. I am not sure whether they swallowed my story or not, but they were kind enough to keep quiet about it, and for the time being they were the only ones who knew about it. But that changed one day when I was filming a scene with Ross, which called for a close-up.

Fortunately Shelley, my make-up artist, was standing behind the director and saw on the monitor that the cameraman had captured the hole.

'You'll have to shoot that again,' she said to the director.

'Sorry?'

'You'll have to re-shoot that.'

'Why?' The director hadn't noticed.

'Because you can see her nose,' she said quietly, pointing to the monitor. 'Danniella's got no nose.' Shelley had wanted to protect me, she hadn't meant to tell anyone my secret, but she had no choice. Either she made the director aware of it and had the scene scrapped or it went out as it was to fifteen million people.

After that the state of my nose became an open secret on set, but Matthew Robinson, an executive on the show, was fantastic. He had a quiet word with the crew and asked them to light me well and only shoot me head on or from above. The cast could not have been more supportive either. None of them said anything to anyone – or even to me. No one treated me any differently. And so it remained a secret for another six months until one fateful night in July, when I was caught off guard by a member of the paparazzi.

11

NOTORIOUS

....

On an evening in the summer of 2000 the full extent of my drug addiction was finally exposed to the public when I was photographed leaving a television awards ceremony by a paparazzo, and from that moment my life changed for ever. The photograph, which made the front pages of nearly every newspaper in the country seven days later, revealed to the nation the secret that so far I, my family, my friends and industry insiders had successfully managed to conceal – that I was, by now, so severely addicted to cocaine and had taken so much of it over the years, that the colonna of my nose had rotted and collapsed.

It was a startling image, one that I find difficult to look at even now, and I am not surprised the media came down on me the way they did. If ever there was a picture to tell a story then this was it, and what a cautionary tale it told. This is what can happen to you if you take drugs, it said. This is what you could end up looking like if you start messing with cocaine. You too could have a gaping hole in your face where your nose should have been, if you dabble in illegal substances.

Once a cover girl for so many teen, celebrity and fashion magazines, once a pin-up for so many faithful fans, overnight I became a poster girl for the dangers of drug abuse. That image and the story of my addiction became the topic of the moment. It was a leading item on the national television news, and it was discussed on the radio. The tabloids hungrily feasted on the story, the broadsheets used it as a peg to discuss the wider implications of drug abuse in today's society. The columnists waded in, wielding their mighty pens. I should be sent to rehab and never be allowed to work in the industry again. I should be made an example of. They accused me of letting down young people all over the land, of sending out the wrong message, of trying to imply that somehow drug abuse was cool. Some wondered how I dared show my face in public looking like that.

More sympathetic writers, of which there were, quite understandably, very few, mused on how and why a once pretty girl with so much to offer could end up this way. Was it indicative of the way we lived today? Was it to do with the pressures of fame and fortune? Were the media themselves somehow to blame? Medical experts were called into television studios to opine on my condition, my addiction and the possibility of reconstructive surgery; drug counsellors were approached to discuss what chances I had of making a recovery. And out of the woodwork crawled my so-called friends and former boyfriends, all eager to tell and sell their version of my story to the Sunday papers for a couple of hundred quid – no doubt to fund their own habits.

And so it went on. From the man in the street to the Right Honourable Member for your local constituency, everyone had an opinion, everyone joined in the debate. My addiction to cocaine and the subsequent damage it caused to my nose became something of a national obsession. I was no longer Danniella Westbrook, the former *EastEnders* star. I was Danniella Westbrook, the girl with no nose.

I was actually undergoing treatment at the Priory hospital, in Roehampton, when the photograph was published. It was my second time in rehab and, unlike the time I went to the Nightingale, this time I really wanted to get clean. I was in the hospital undergoing a treatment programme that lasted 28 days and I really wanted it to work for me. The Soap Awards had taken place seven days earlier and I guess the photographer hadn't initially noticed what he had captured in that picture when he filed his snaps to his picture desk that night. It was probably only when he went to bin the rejects later on that he realised what he had. But when he did he made sure copies went to every newspaper in the country.

I didn't see the papers that morning. At the Priory we were discouraged from reading them, and though there was no official ban on looking at them I guess that when the doctors and nurses there saw the front pages of the papers that day they must have decided to keep them away from me in case I got upset. But what they hadn't banked on was the fact that it would be on the television as well. And so as I was sitting there that morning, feeling depressed and worn down by the fact that I was in rehab again, I decided to tune in to *The Big Breakfast* to cheer myself up. What a mistake that was.

It was like watching a car crash happen in front of my eyes. When I tuned in Johnny Vaughn, the show's presenter, was holding up a copy of the *Sun* and laughing. I moved closer to the television to see what was so funny and then I saw it. I saw the photo. I saw the picture of me stumbling out of the National Soap Awards after the show party looking 'tired and emotional', and poking my tongue out at the press – and then I saw my nose.

I sat there unable to move.

I don't recall what Johnny was saying; I don't think I took it in. All I could hear was the sound of the studio audience laughing – laughing at me, laughing at the hole in my nose. Johnny's co-presenter Denise Van Outen leapt to my defence. She had been at Sylvia's with me and we had been good friends. 'Leave her alone, Johnny,' she said. 'She's a lovely girl and I wish

her all the best. Let's hope she makes a good recovery.'
It was kind of her to fight my corner. She didn't have
to, but it had little effect anyway. Johnny and the rest
of the studio just kept on laughing.

I remember sitting there clutching my head in my
hands, rocking backwards and forwards, staring into
the distance. 'Oh God,' I thought. 'What have I done
to myself? What have I done? I am nothing more than a
national joke. I am nothing more than a laughing
stock.'

Drug addiction is never just one person's story. It
always involves a cast of characters who end up with
starring roles in the addict's real-life soap opera,
whether they like it or not. In my own woeful drama
I managed to cast four generations of my family, from
my grandmother, to my parents, to my brothers Justin
and Jay, to my son Kai and later, my daughter Jodie. I
am not proud of that fact. Indeed, it is now one of my
most profound regrets. It is bad enough that I had to
ruin my own life through my addiction. It is worse that
I had to include those people, the ones who loved and
cared for me most, and take them down with me.

The publication of the photograph had caused me a
great deal of anxiety and distress, but I had only myself
to blame. If I was being ridiculed by press and public
alike, then so be it. I was fair game. It was what I
deserved. But for my family it was different. They
hadn't asked to be put into that position. They hadn't

wanted it. None of them was in the public eye, or wanted to be. Whilst I had always craved the limelight, hungered for fame and public accolade, they had lived their lives in private, seeking nothing more than love and respect from people who were close to them, people who mattered. But my very public battle with drug addiction made them all unwitting players in my story.

I was lucky in that I was closeted away at the Priory when the picture was published – although, of course, I didn't see it like that at the time. But as much as I hated being in rehab, at least in that environment the press couldn't get to me. In fact they had no idea where I was, and the hospital certainly weren't going to tell them. But for my family it was another matter. Unable to find out where I was, the press turned their attention to my parents, door-stepping them at home and at work, harassing them with calls and letters requesting interviews. They wanted to know my story; they wanted to know how bad my addiction really was; they wanted to know about my nose and what it was like being related to me – a stupid question really, as it must have been terrible for my family, especially during that time.

It was pretty tough on my brothers, too. When my older brother Justin, who had worked so hard and diligently for his position in the City, arrived at his office that morning he found a newspaper cutting of the photograph attached to his computer. Next to it was a Post-it note, on which was written one word: junkie. When he left his desk later on that day to go for lunch, the same thing happened. People made snide remarks to him about me throughout the afternoon. They laughed about me, made cheap jokes about my nose and my coke problem. It was hard for Justin, not least because, as my older brother, he had always looked out for me. Had someone made a disparaging remark like that about me in a pub, or out at dinner, he probably would have punched their lights out. But at work he was completely defenceless. There was nothing he could say or do. He just had to take it on the chin.

As for Jay, well, when you are trying to forge a career for yourself in the police force, being related to the most famous drug addict in the country is never going to be helpful. It was really hard for him during the weeks that followed, and I am sure that there were moments when he simply wished that I had never been born.

There is no question that my addiction to cocaine caused a rift between my brothers and me. Justin and I didn't grow up with each other, but from our teenage years we were as thick as thieves. When I bought my first flat, he bought one below me, we were that close. We shared the same outlook, the same sense of humour and for a time we shared the same friends. But when I started taking coke he couldn't cope with it all. My brother liked to have a good time, he knew how to party, but he didn't like to think of his little sister screwing up her life because of drugs. It was one thing me going out and having a good time, quite another that I was a drug addict.

'You don't have to do that, Danni,' he used to say to me. 'Just come out and have a drink and a laugh.'

But of course I never listened. I just thought he was being over-protective and wished at times that he would loosen up a little.

Because Jay was eight years younger than me, I didn't have the same kinds of problem with him but, looking back on that time now, it was probably harder for him than it was for Justin. Jay was still just a child when I became heavily involved with drugs, still a little boy, no older than my own son is now. And he had to shoulder the worst of those times. He was still living at home, so he heard the conversations and the arguments between my parents and me, and he witnessed the fights. When my parents should have been looking out for him, they had to contend with my issues. When, by the time I had moved out, they should have been concentrating on him, they had to look out for me. When the photograph of me appeared in the papers he was still at school and so had to deal with all that. I know that both my addiction and my behaviour denied Jay a lot of his childhood. And I know that I forced him to grow up before his time.

It was hard for my grandmother as well. I don't think Nan really understood what was going on or what it all meant. All that she knew was that I was really sick and was destroying my life, and that no matter what anyone did or said, no one seemed to be able to help me. It's difficult for an older generation to sit back and watch a younger one do that to themselves. When I was a child, she had always been so full of hope for me, so supportive and encouraging. And now in her twilight years, when she should have been enjoying her granddaughter's achievements, she had to watch me blow it all away.

It was difficult for all of them. They had had to live with my addiction for such a long time, and although I treated them all badly over the years they always supported me and protected me. They tried to keep my problems and issues within the family. They tried to hide the extent of my addiction from the outside world. They kept the state of my nose to themselves, as a secret that should never get out. But now it had. And not only did everyone know about it, but everyone was talking about it too.

In the aftermath of the publication of the photograph you couldn't open a paper without seeing some article about it; you couldn't listen to the radio without hearing some debate or phone-in on the subject; you couldn't switch on the television without someone taking a swipe at me. Chris Evans, Frank Skinner, Jonathan Ross, Angus Deayton, the top presenters of the time, all had a go. Sure, it hurt me a great deal, not least because I was trying to get clean at the time, but I didn't really have a leg to stand on. I had it brought it all on myself. But for my family it was different. It upset them to hear their daughter, their granddaughter, their sister, spoken about in that way. I may have deserved it all, but I was still their flesh and blood and so it wounded them deeply.

But in the greater scheme of things this was only a flashpoint, a moment, in their lives. Their problems with me had of course been going on for a great many years before that, from the moment I started becoming addicted to cocaine.

Although my parents would both deny that my addiction to cocaine had anything to do with their divorce, there is no question in my mind that the pressure I put them under during those years must have contributed in some shape or form to the breakdown of their marriage.

My addiction and behaviour were a constant source of worry and concern for them both, and though they dealt with it all in very different ways they were united in their shared sense of hurt, disappointment, shame and fear.

And then, of course, there was the guilt that they felt. Although, as I have said, I had no one to blame for my problems but myself, my parents didn't see it that way. It may not be right, but it is quite natural for parents to lay the blame on themselves when their children go off the rails, and I know that there were times when my mother and father looked at me and thought: 'Where did we go wrong?' It was, of course, ridiculous of them to do so. They had only ever given me the best in life, and in any case there is only so much you can do as a parent to protect your kids from the big bad world, but they just couldn't help blaming themselves.

My mother always says that her marriage came to a natural end, but I am not so sure. It wasn't just the public humiliation I caused them; it wasn't just the fact that their daughter was a known junkie; it was also the personal problems I brought them as well. I forced them to live on the edge, I caused them countless sleepless nights, and I created a tension in their marriage, which I don't believe was there before. I know there were nights when my parents would like awake in bed waiting for that call to say that I was in trouble, that I was in hospital, or that I was dead.

When they did finally separate, I admit that at times, instead of being contrite or even sympathetic about what had happened, I used their split for my own ends. I remember one fight with my mother, about my addiction, ending on the taunt: 'I'm not surprised your marriage ended. I wouldn't have put up with your nagging!'

Between the ages of twenty-one and twenty-five my relationship with my parents was very off and on. Whenever I thought they were interfering in my life I would stop having contact for a while, returning to them when I needed help and, later on, money. I had avoided them when I was out of work and living in Buckhurst Hill for a time, and I didn't speak to them for a couple of months after they put me into the Nightingale. We patched up our differences when Kai was born and then fell out again later on. It was a pattern we maintained until the time that I eventually stopped taking drugs.

My estrangements from my father were never particularly dramatic. When it got to the point when he could no longer deal with me, we simply stopped calling each other or seeing each other. It just hurt him so much to see me that way. And if I am honest, it was easier for me not to see him as well during those periods. He was the one person who made me feel truly guilty about what I had become, about my addiction. I was finding it increasingly hard to carry on living the life I was and to look him in the eye. There was no big fight or row that ever came between us – we just lost contact for a while.

With my mother it was always far more dramatic. There was always a fight or a scene that would act as a catalyst for our fall-outs. I could be very vicious with her, and whilst she could at times give as good as she got and talk back to me, there were times when it all became too much. Sometimes I would get physically aggressive with her. If we were having a row and she wouldn't do what I wanted, like give me access to my savings, for example, I would start to kick and scream until I got her attention. I'd grab her by the arm or on one occasion by the neck and shout at her until I had got her attention. On one of these occasions, realising that I wasn't going to change, and was never going to listen to her or do anything to help myself, she decided that she had to walk away for while. Although she still loved me she realised that we both needed some distance, some time apart from one another. Following her divorce she bought a house, and when it came to signing the deeds for it, she did so using her maiden name: Sue Maynard. Up to that point she had been happy to carry on using the name Westbrook, but she was now fed up with all the negative attention that came with sharing surname with her wayward daughter. She wasn't trying to disown me, she just needed a break and some space. She was tired of the phone calls from the press and thought that by reverting to her old name she might be able to escape them for a while. But the significance of this move was not lost on me. It struck me as deeply ironic that the one person in my family who had once been so proud to be related to Danniella Westbrook was now so ashamed of that relationship that she had felt forced to change her name.

12
TRUE LOVE

....

I said earlier that I didn't want to go into detail about my past relationships because I honestly don't believe that any of them were relevant to what happened to me in the long run. But there is one person in my life who I cannot fail to mention in the story of my addiction and that is Kevin Jenkins, the man I would eventually have the good fortune to marry and the person who was ultimately responsible for saving my life.

I met Kevin in November 1999 at the Kensington Gardens Hotel, in West London. It was during my third and final stint on *EastEnders*, just a couple of months before I left the soap for good. I had been invited out for the evening by Michael Grecco, the actor who played Beppe di Marco, my on-screen love interest. Off screen Michael and I were nothing more than friends, but we were incredibly close and spent a lot of time together away from the set. The night Kevin and I met, Michael had invited me to a boxing event at the hotel and I had been really looking forward to it. I loved being with Michael, who was always so sound and such a support to me. For some reason he was one of the few people I would listen to when it came to telling me off about my drug use.

'Come on, Danni,' he'd say. 'You don't have to do that stuff. It's not good for you and I like you the way you are without it.'

Michael and I were having a good time together laughing, talking and drinking at our table, when a mutual friend introduced me to Kevin. He was tall and very handsome and there was an intensity in his eyes that instantly drew me to him. As soon as we were introduced he sat down next to me and we began to talk. I liked him immediately. He was warm and funny and we just clicked straight away. He was unlike anyone I had met before. He seemed so strong and confident, so sure of who he was, and he had every right to be.

At the age of thirty-two Kevin was a successful businessman, who ran a company called Premier, which is one of London's leading courier and security companies. He had built the company up from scratch, from a tiny room in Waterloo with just one bike, into a business that now had offices and drivers all over the capital. He was at the event that night because Premier were handling the security for the evening.

I admired him for his hard-won success. For too long I had been hanging out with people who either had it all simply by virtue of being a celebrity or did nothing with their lives whatsoever. It was like a breath of fresh air to meet someone like Kevin. Someone who had worked hard and steadily for everything he had, and had really achieved something with his life.

We spent the rest of the evening locked in conversation, unable to tear ourselves away from one another. 'This is the kind of man I should be with,' I thought to myself. 'This is the kind of person I need.' My attraction to Kevin was reciprocated. He flirted with me throughout the night, paying me compliments, sometimes fleetingly brushing his hand against my knee. At one point in the evening he leant over and whispered in my ear, 'I'm going to marry you.'

I knew right away that I wanted to be with Kevin, but I was hesitant. He had been married before and I wasn't sure what the state of play was with that relationship.

'I don't date married men,' I told him when he asked whether he could see me again.

'But I'm not,' he said, explaining that his marriage had ended.

I was still hesitant. 'When I know for sure that you are on your own, when I know that there is no one else in your life, then I'll have dinner with you,' I said. Although Kevin was unable to arrange a date for dinner with me, he wasn't going to let me walk out of his life that night for ever. So he found another way of making sure he would see me again.

I had been involved at that time in a legal dispute with my ex-husband and was due to go to court the following week for a hearing. We hadn't parted on the best of terms and I was worried about having to come face to face with him in court. Because Kevin knew my ex-husband, that night I mentioned to him that I was worried about it.

'Don't you worry about a thing. You don't have to go through this on your own,' he said to me as I was saying goodbye to him that night. 'I'll make sure you have all the support you need. I'll see to it myself and I'll be there for you.'

I was really bowled over by this gesture. I was used to men flirting with me and trying to chat me up. It was an occupational hazard, I guess. I was also used to people trying to befriend me just because of who I was, or because of what I could give them. But I wasn't used to this. Here, in front of me, was a man offering me support and friendship, despite the fact I had just turned him down for a date.

'You'd really do that for me?' I asked.

'Of course I would,' he said. 'Let's meet next week and make a plan of action.'

And so, one week later, on the evening before I was due to appear in court, I met with Kevin for an early evening drink at the Fire Station bar, in Waterloo. I had played hard to get when he had asked me out for dinner at the boxing match, but when he had offered to support me through my court appearance I admit that he really got to me. In the days that followed I couldn't get him out of my mind. I knew I was going to see him in a week's time, but it was beginning to feel like an eternity, so I managed to get his mobile phone number from a mutual friend. I think he was surprised to hear from me, but certainly not unhappy about it, and in the days before we met again we had a number of quite flirty conversations.

When we met that evening there was such a sense of ease between us. It was as though we had known each other for years. When Kevin had run through the itinerary for the next day, and booked cars to take me to and from the court, he turned to me and said: 'How about that dinner then?'

'OK,' I said. 'I'll have dinner with you.'

'Well, let's go . . .'

'You mean tonight?'

'Yes, tonight. Why not?'

It only took me a second to make up my mind. As Kevin had said – why not?

The concept of soul mates had always appealed to me. I had always liked the idea that there is someone for everyone, that there are people who are destined to be with each other and that there is one person in this world who is totally right for you. In my early teens I hoped that I would one day find mine and we would marry and live happily ever after, but by my mid-twenties I was beginning to give up on the idea and see it as nothing more than a dream.

I had been let down by a lot of people in the past, I had been hurt and I just couldn't seem, as much as I tried, to find the right person. My addiction to drugs hadn't helped. It's not easy to form a sincere relationship with someone, and give it your all, when all you are really ever thinking about is your next fix. And it's difficult to love anyone when you are in that state of mind, going from high to low, suffering from violent mood swings.

And then, of course, there was the fact that I had Kai. From the moment I had Kai I loved him so much that I didn't really believe I was capable of loving anyone else. I had tried twice – once with his father and then with my ex-husband – to have a relationship in order to give my son some security in his life. But when both those relationships failed I realised that rather than helping Kai all I was doing was creating more problems for him. I didn't want him to get attached to someone if it wasn't going to work out, I wanted to spare him that kind of pain.

But when I met Kevin I knew that I had found 'the one'. I knew that he was right for me, there was just something about him. He made me feel secure and happy in myself right from the word go. Unlike my other past boyfriends, Kevin was a real man. He wasn't gauche, he wasn't young, and he wasn't naïve. He lived his own life, one that he had built for himself, he had his own views and opinions, and he wasn't scared to voice them.

He wasn't interested in the fact that I was an actress, he didn't, and still to this day doesn't, understand all the fuss about that world. In fact, if we have one source of tension within our relationship then I would say it was that. Kevin just doesn't care about that industry, he doesn't get the whole fame game. At the time his attitude just made me like him even more. I had spent too much time being surrounded by sycophants who only wanted a piece of me because of what I was and what I could give them. Now I had met someone who liked me for who I really was, and at once that made me feel secure and comfortable.

Another reason why I liked Kevin was that he had a child of his own. His daughter Jordan was a couple of years older than Kai, and the way he spoke of her during our first few dates together made me realise just how much she meant to him. I knew that Kevin, unlike other men I had met, would never make me compromise my relationship with my son to be with him. I knew that he would never compete for Kai's attention, nor treat him as a nuisance. Kevin didn't see the fact that I had a child as baggage – he knew, being in the position himself, that it was just part of the picture. If he wanted to be with me, then he would have to want to be with Kai too. And if I wanted to be with him, then I would have to want to be with Jordan.

Kevin was aware that I used coke during the initial stages of our romance, but for him then it wasn't a big deal. He knew I liked to party and he was used to hanging out with quite a fast and hard-living group of people. It certainly wasn't unusual for people in that world to do drugs, and so during our first few weeks together it really wasn't an issue. As far as he was concerned I took the drug socially and that was that. It didn't occur to him then I was using all day, every day.

I had left Kai with my mother while I went to meet Kevin at the Fire Station, thinking I was only going to be out for a couple of hours. Now Kevin was on the telephone to her asking if she would mind looking after him while we had dinner. She agreed to take him for the night. I think she was so thrilled that I was going on a proper dinner date and with someone who had the good grace to ring and ask her such a thing – that she was happy to help. We went for dinner at TGI's in Enfield. I'm not sure why we went there, by that stage I didn't care where I was going. All that mattered to me then was that I was with him. After dinner as his driver ferried us back to his house we had our first tentative kiss and from that moment we were inseparable. I stayed with him that night and never went home after that. I moved in with him the following day but, as intense and sudden as our relationship was, it was a while before we slept together. I think that we were both so desperate for things to work out between us, for it to develop into something more, that we were scared of ruining it. We wanted to find our feet as a couple, to let our relation-ship reach a higher level before we took that step. And so for those first few weeks together we just lay in bed like a couple of love-struck, nervous teenagers, watching videos, eating chocolate and occasionally kissing and holding hands. When eventually we did take our relationship further, Kevin turned to me afterwards and said, 'You know, I really respect you, Danni.' It's funny but that has always stuck with me. I don't why. I guess no one had ever said that to me before, and until he said it I had no idea how much it would matter to me. I wasn't used to being treated like this. I wasn't used to someone caring for me in this way.

Kevin was as good as his word and supported me through the court case that finalised my divorce. Then three blissful weeks later, he proposed to me on a flight to Florida. He had booked a surprise holiday to Disney World and we were sitting in First Class drinking champagne. I can't remember what we were talking about, but suddenly Kevin stood up and took my hand, and then went down on one knee in the aisle.

'I love you, Danni,' he said. 'I love you and I want to marry you. Will you, will you marry me?'

I couldn't believe what I was hearing. It was all so sudden. But deep within me I knew that it was right and I knew that more than anything in the world I wanted to marry him too.

'Yes,' I said. 'Yes. I love you too. I'll marry you!'

I can't remember if I laughed or cried after that, although I do recall the air stewardesses and other passengers clapping and cheering. All I know was that I was overcome by this feeling of intense euphoria and love. I felt safe and wanted. As I sat next to him, his hand in mine, I thought 'this is the happiest moment of my life', and even though I was in my Virgin Atlantic pyjamas, I can safely say that it was the most romantic moment of my entire life.

When I met Kevin in November I was still working on *EastEnders*, but within just a couple of months of being with him I was out of the soap once again. I wasn't fired this time, but let's just say that when they gave me the opportunity to walk I took it. I was no longer interested in acting and that had become blatantly obvious to everyone on set. The soap was now being shown four times a week and it was impossible to balance the workload with my addiction. While I was at work Kai attended nursery and although I didn't go out that much in the evenings I was still using at home at night. Come the morning I would feel terrible, and once again it was beginning to have an effect on my performances.

'Why are you doing this to yourself? Why do you do that stuff?' Michael Grecco would say to me. Michael has always been vehemently anti-drugs and just couldn't understand it. Not only had it destroyed my nose, but it was about to destroy my career again as well.

'You know, I love working with you,' he said. 'Why

do you want to put your career in the balance like that. You've got a kid to support.' Michael was always covering for me when I was late or I forgot my lines, but he knew that the producers were tiring of my behaviour.

'Danni, if they let you go again, it will be your last time,' he said. Prophetic words.

When I did leave the production at the end of 1999 it was in fact a fairly mutual decision. I admit that had I begged the producers to let me stay this time I doubt if they would have allowed me to. But I was happy to go. I had met Kevin by now and decided that all I wanted to do with my time was to be with him and Kai.

I didn't feel anything when I left – no sadness, no remorse. Looking back to that point now it fills me with shame that I could have behaved in that way and let down so many people who were all doing everything they could to help me. It wasn't just that I was wasting their time on set. Outside work too they had all bent over backwards to protect me, and they had made sure that the state of my nose or the extent of my drug addiction didn't get out – and this is how I had repaid them.

Kevin had known a bit about my problems when we started going out. Even if you weren't interested in the celebrity world or a soap fan it was hard not to have heard something of my story by then. By that stage I no longer had a nose, but somehow none of that bothered him. He took me as I was and never judged me. He took me on, he loved me, I loved him and that was all that mattered.

For his family, however, it was quite another story. They simply couldn't understand what he was doing with me, why he would want to date, let alone marry, a girl with my kind of history. My addiction to cocaine was well documented, they knew all about it and they didn't want him to be associated with someone like me. And so they gave him an ultimatum. It was me or them – and when he chose to be with me, all of them apart from his mother broke off contact with him for good.

So despite our intense love for each other I wouldn't say it was the easiest start to a relationship. Nevertheless, we managed to get through it all. One of the reasons for this was that we were always, as a couple, able to see past all our issues and demons and take each other for who we really were. For Kevin that meant seeing me as a person and not just a cocaine addict. For me that meant looking at my fiancé and seeing him as the kind and sensitive man I knew him to be rather than a ruthless businessman, hell-bent on getting a deal. Because of the world he was in, one that involved security and protection, Kevin dealt with some quite shady characters. I remember coming home with him one night after we had spent the evening in the company of some of this crowd and saying to him: 'Why do you hang out with people like that? Why do you spend your time with gangsters? You're not like that as a person.' And he just turned to me and smiled. He was pleased that I could see the real him.

When we returned from our first holiday in Florida, Kevin presented me with a beautiful diamond engagement ring from Tiffany's, but although we knew we wanted to be together for ever neither of us was in a particular hurry to walk down the aisle again. We just wanted to enjoy our engagement and have a good time together, and for a while that's exactly what we did. We lived a glamorous, high-octane, life together, going from party to party. And for a time it was good fun. But after six months of living like that it all got a bit too much for Kevin and he couldn't stand the pace any longer. He had done all that when he was young and single, and now he was bored with it. He had tired of that world – of going out, of drinking every night and, lately, of me getting high. And now that he had found me and made a commitment to me, all he wanted was just to be with me and the children and settle down, but he knew that was only going to be possible if we turned our backs on that life.

It was Kevin who suggested that I went to the Priory in the summer of 2000. It had nothing to with the publication of the photograph of me leaving the Soap Awards. Kevin was simply concerned about the amount of cocaine I was taking. Although he could always see past my addiction problems and take me for what I really was, he was beginning to worry that the drugs were actually making me ill. He could also see the detrimental effect they were having on our relationship. We always had a very easy-going relationship and were very much in love, but if we stayed out late and I was hung over or coming down the next day, I could be tetchy and difficult and we would often argue.

So for the sake of our relationship – and his own sanity – Kevin recommended that I should go into treatment at the Priory and offered to pay for it. The course would last twenty-eight days and the aim was that when I came out I would be clean and on my way to recovery. Now when I had gone into rehab the first time, at the Nightingale, I didn't want to recover. I liked taking drugs, and had no intention of stopping. But this time round it was different. I still liked drugs and I didn't really want to stop taking them, but given a choice between a life taking cocaine and being with the man I loved, I knew what I had to do.

I am not going to say that it was easy, because it wasn't. It was really hard and there were times when I wanted out. The incident with the photograph caused me quite a severe setback, but the therapists there were good to me. I thought about cocaine every day I was in there, fantasised about taking it again and couldn't imagine living life without it, but I did my best. Kevin was a huge support and came to see me every day, attending counselling sessions and the friends and family group meetings.

'You can do it, Danni, you really can,' he'd say to

me when he left me each day, and after a while I began to believe him.

When I had completed my twenty-eight days Kevin whisked me off to Palm Island, in Barbados, for a romantic break. It was his way of congratulating me for getting through it, of coming out the other side. Kevin had planned the trip as a surprise for me, but unfortunately I seemed to be the only person who was in the dark about it. The tabloid press, who had been desperate to find me ever since the truth about my nose had been exposed, had been tipped off about our aeroplane booking, and when we arrived in Barbados the airport was swarming with paps. I was, understandably, very upset. Fortunately, because we were flying on to an exclusive resort in Palm Island, we were able to shake most of them off, but there was one particularly tenacious photographer who managed to get wind of where we were off to. His name was Jason Fraser. It turned out that he had flown over to Palm Island on the same flight as us. I had even seen him on the flight but didn't for one moment suspect that he was a photographer, because he was with his girlfriend and they just looked like any other couple. But on our second day on the island there was a knock at the door of our hotel bungalow.

'Sorry to bother you,' he said. 'My name is Jason Fraser.'

He didn't have to finish the sentence, for I knew

exactly who he was. Jason was one of the most famous paparazzi in the world, who had made a name for himself when he took the photographs of the Princess of Wales and Dodi Fayed holidaying in the South of France shortly before she died.

'Could I have a minute?' he asked.

Jason explained that he had watched us for a couple of days and that he had seen that I was well and happy. He said that he didn't want to intrude but that there was such a huge interest in my story at the time that there were photographers crawling all over the place trying to get the first picture of me since the exposé.

'Why don't I take a picture of you to put an end to the story once and for all?' he suggested. 'It will show you looking happy and well and they'll all leave you alone then.'

I thought about it for a while and decided that it was a good idea. Maybe that way Kevin and I could get back to normal and enjoy the rest of our holiday. And so the following day I allowed Jason to photograph me with Kevin. The pictures appeared in the papers the next day, along with a story about how I had got clean. Jason was right: after that we were left alone by the other paps, but we did spend a lot of time with Jason in the following days and I now consider him to be a close friend.

The rest of the holiday was pure bliss and I couldn't have felt better. I was healthy and happy and it felt wonderful. I didn't think I was going to be able to do it this time, but I had, and when I was out there on the island with Kevin, drugs couldn't have been further from my mind. I didn't have them. I didn't want them or need them. All I wanted was to be like this for ever with the man I loved.

'I'm so proud of you, Danni,' Kevin said to me one evening as we looked out to sea. 'I really think we can make this work and be happy from now on.' And I thought so too. I really believed at that moment that this was a new beginning for us both.

We flew back to London two weeks later, and when we landed at Heathrow Kevin said that we would have to make our separate ways back into town. Not only did he have to go straight to the office to make sure everything with his business was OK, but he wanted to go and spend some time with his mother who was very ill with cancer. Kevin had always been close to her, and when he started seeing me she was the one person in his family who refused to get involved. So long as he was happy she didn't mind who he saw, and she carried on seeing him.

The plan was that I would go back to the Conrad Hotel, in Chelsea Harbour, where we were staying, and wait for him there.

'You'll be OK, won't you?' he said, kissing me. 'Go to the hotel, have a nice bath, relax, unpack. I'll only be a couple of hours.'

'Sure,' I said as he got into a cab. 'I'll be fine. You

don't need to worry about me, just go and do your thing.'

But Kevin did need to worry about me. As I got into my taxi, asking the driver to take me to Chelsea, I suddenly began to panic. I couldn't bear the thought of being away from him all afternoon. I couldn't stand the idea of being alone, in my own company, for those hours. For the past six weeks Kevin hadn't left my side. I thought I had come to terms with my recovery, but all that had been in an extremely closeted world. If I wasn't in the Priory being treated and cared for, then I had been with Kevin, on a paradise island, away from temptation. But now I was back and alone in the big bad world, and there it was staring me in the face, calling to me, and I just couldn't help myself.

I took my mobile from my bag and scrolled through the names of my so-called friends. I rang a number.

'What are you doing this afternoon?' I asked when the person at the other end picked up the phone. 'Fancy hanging out for a couple of hours?'

And as soon as she said she did, I told the driver there had been a change of plan.

When I eventually turned up at the hotel it was past two in the morning. Kevin was sitting on the bed with his head in his hands. He didn't have to look at me to know what I had been doing. He didn't have to speak to me to know that I was off my head. From the moment that he arrived at the hotel early that evening, ready to take me for dinner, and found that I wasn't there, he knew. He had tried to call me, but I had switched off my phone. He had tried to track me down, but after a while he just gave up.

He wasn't angry with me, he was beyond that. He was simply heartbroken. He just couldn't understand how I could, after everything we had been through together, do that to him, to myself and to us.

13

THROWING IT ALL AWAY

....

Kevin, quite understandably, didn't want to have anything to do with me after that, and so we broke up. It was July 2000. It wasn't because he fell out of love with me, he just felt that he couldn't be around me any more. My behaviour that night had seen to that. I had pushed him too far. He had wanted so much for us to build a life together, to have a fresh start, but I just couldn't do it. I couldn't stop myself from putting my addiction to cocaine before anything else, even our relationship. My time in treatment had obviously meant nothing to me, it seemed to him. The holiday in Palm Island, the things we talked about when we were there, the plans we made for the future – it was as though it had all been one big charade to me, as though I was just going through the motions to humour him. And that really hurt Kevin.

I may not have really wanted to stay clean and sober, but he did. It was through my own addiction to drugs that Kevin realised that he had his own problem with alcohol. During my time in the Priory Kevin had been there for me: he had come to therapy with me, had listened to the counsellors and read the literature on drug dependency that I had been given. And through his attempt to understand my disease he realised that he had one of his own.

Because of the world he mixed in Kevin drank quite heavily. It's what those people did. It wasn't just a case of having a nice glass of wine or a beer once or twice a week after work. If he was out with that group he'd start early and carry on drinking throughout the night until we went home, which was often quite late. Before we went away he was beginning to notice that it was having an effect on his personality and that if he was out he felt uncomfortable without a drink in his hand. And so he decided that he was going to give up drinking for good and checked himself in for a month-long stay at the Priory.

Kevin, being the kind of man he is, took the treatment very seriously. It was his mission and he was going to get everything he could from it. After being there just a couple of weeks he saw that it was possible for him to live without alcohol, and when he left after twenty-eight days he was sober. He was determined to stay that way, but he knew that if he was to succeed he couldn't see me – not until I had addressed my own demons.

And so we went our separate ways. I moved with

Kai into a house that Kevin rented in Orpington, Kent, and he went to stay with his parents. Kevin's mother was by now very seriously ill and he wanted to be there for her and give her as much attention as he could while she was still alive. He didn't want any other distractions in his life at this time, and he certainly didn't need any trouble from me.

Naturally, I was distraught. I couldn't believe that I had done this to myself – and to Kai as well. For a time I had had it all, a beautiful life, with a handsome and adoring fiancé, who was only too happy to act as a father figure to my child. I had found a man who was prepared to take me on, to love me unconditionally and give me a life that I never thought possible. I had met someone who wanted to take me away from the world of drugs and do anything he could, no matter what it cost either financially or emotionally, to try and get me clean, and I had just thrown it all away. For what? For some seedy little night out with a so-called friend and a couple of grams of white powder.

This, of course, was another of those moments when I should have learnt my lesson, but I am ashamed to say that I not only carried on using but started taking more drugs than I had ever done before, sometimes using as much as ten grams a day. All I can say in my defence is that I was desperately miserable and low, and I felt more reliant on drugs than ever.

The vast quantity of drugs I was taking, combined with the anguish and distress I was feeling at losing

Kevin, were having a profound effect on my mental state, and it was around this time that I started to behave psychotically. I became obsessed with Kevin and fixated on getting him back. When Kevin refused to take my calls on his mobile I would ring his parents' house day and night, sometimes as late as three in the morning. If his father answered I would scream at him demanding to speak to Kevin, at other times I would slam the phone down. Quite understandably Kevin's father resented me. He was having to cope with his wife dying, trying to hold it together for the sake of her and his family, and the last thing he needed was this drug-fuelled mad girl ringing at all times of the night.

Kevin decided that the only way forward was to keep in contact with me. Though he was paying for Kai and me to live in his Orpington house he was reluctant to give me any cash, fearing I would just spend it on more drugs, and so from time to time he would call round with groceries for us. It was his way of doing his bit, making sure I was OK and seeing Kai, to whom he had by now become very close. One afternoon Kevin called me and said that he would be round that evening with my shopping. He would drive to see me after he had attended an Alcoholics Anonymous meeting in London. I was pleased. I was looking forward to seeing him and was counting down the hours until he would be with me again. But Kevin's meeting was running late. Unable to reach me, he told his driver to take the groceries round to me and to let me know that he would be there just as soon as he could once the session had ended. As he went into the meeting he switched his mobile off. When Kevin didn't arrive at my house I began to panic. I called him but there was no answer. I tried again, and again, and again.

'He's not coming! He's lied to me, he's out with someone else.' These thoughts just kept running through my head. I took some coke to steady myself, them some more. I had a drink and tried calling him again. By now I was crazed out my head. I went to the bathroom and took every pill I could find from the medicine cabinet – Nurofen, paracetamols, cold and flu remedies – poured a large glass of water and downed them. 'That will show him!' I thought.

By the time the driver arrived – maybe half an hour later – the pills had taken effect. He rang the doorbell several times but there was no answer, and so he rang Kevin's office. Kevin had just come out of the meeting and was listening to the abusive messages I had left him when the man got through to him. By the time he had made the journey from London to Orpington it must have been just after 11 p.m. He broke into the house and ran up the stairs to find me slumped on my bed semi-conscious. He shook me awake.

'Danni, Danni!' he shouted, trying to get a reaction from me. When I came round he was on the phone calling an ambulance. He was talking to the response service, going through the names on the bottles and packets of pills, telling them what I had taken. There were a couple of extra pills left on the bedside table.

'Well, you can't have meant to kill yourself, otherwise you would have taken them all,' he said to me, pointing to them as he put the phone down.

'Oh yeah? Is that right? Watch me!' And with that, like the selfish idiot I was, I grabbed them, put them in my mouth and swallowed them.

Determined that I would stay conscious, Kevin put me in the shower while he waited for help to arrive. He then called his brother Barry and arranged for him to stay in the house with Kai.

When I woke I was lying in a hospital bed at Queen Mary's, Orpington. By my bedside were Kevin, his friend Luc, and my father. As soon as I had been admitted Kevin had called Dad and told him what had happened. The two men had always got on well together and were close. As soon as Dad heard he rushed to my bedside.

'It can't go on like this,' Dad had said to Kevin while they waited for me to come round.

'I know, I know,' said Kevin.

'What are we going to do with her?'

'I'm not sure what choices we have left.'

Kevin and Dad spoke to the doctors and talked about the possibility of having me sectioned. It wasn't an easy conversation for any of them. Whatever I had done they still loved me, but they just couldn't see a way out of the situation. Having me sectioned was extreme, but what were they to do? My overdose might just have been a cry for help this time, but what about the next time? They felt they just couldn't risk it. I needed help. The doctor explained to them that they would have to wait until I came round, because they would have to assess me. But when I did and found out what was happening I was having none of it. I switched in to actress mode and during the consultation, while Kevin and my father were out of the room, I convinced him that I was OK.

'Look, I'm just a bit distressed at the moment,' I said. 'I've had a bad time splitting up with my boyfriend and I've had flu. It was nothing serious, I was just feeling sorry for myself.'

I think the doctor was relieved. They didn't want to section me. I would have had to stay there and they were probably worried about the adverse publicity that would follow if it got leaked to the press.

When I was discharged a few days later I went to stay with Dad, who by now was living in Islington with his new girlfriend. Everyone decided it was for the best. I couldn't be trusted to be on my own, and this way Dad could keep an eye on me and look after Kai. But I left after a couple of weeks. I couldn't stay there for ever and I had to try and get on and live my own life. Though he had supported me through that incident, Kevin understandably still wasn't ready to get back together with me, and so I had to move on and stand on my own two feet for the first time in ages.

*   *   *

From the moment I had moved in with him Kevin had taken care of me and always supported me. We had lived in a succession of lovely houses from a luxurious penthouse in Brighton Marina to a beautiful five-bedroom Georgian house in Windsor. Kevin made sure that Kai and I didn't want for anything. Even when we had broken up in July of that year he had made sure I was OK, putting me up in the town house in Orpington. But that situation had suddenly come to an end, and it was up to me to find Kai and me somewhere to live.

The problem was I had managed to lose somewhere in the region of a million pounds. Rather than invest the money I had earned from the sale of the flat in Buckhurst Hill I used it to live on and rented property instead until I moved in with Kevin. So I had foolishly managed to lose the one good thing that had come out of my career – the roof over my head. And on top of that, of course, I had been spending a huge amount of money every week on coke.

I made a small amount of money from re-runs of *EastEnders*, but it certainly wasn't enough to fund the extravagant lifestyle I was used to. There were to be no penthouses for me and Kai, no nice Georgian homes either. It was going to be a struggle for me to pay the rent on a one-bedroom flat, let alone deal with its running costs.

While I had been with Kevin my relationship with my parents had improved. My father adored him and

DANNIELLA WESTBROOK
as Sam Mitchell

EastEnders
BBC ONE

Back on the Square. This was taken during my last stint
on the show, in 1999.

Filming Ross Kemp's leaving scene with 'Super Beps', Michael Grecco, a great actor and a great mate.

A night out at the Atlantic Bar. I'm wired, Kevin's stressed.

Day release from the Priory, doing some shopping therapy – the only kind I was interested in at the time.

Me and Luc at Gatwick, in 2001, on our way to treatment in Arizona. I was three months pregnant and seriously ill.

Tired, but in recovery. I was about to leave Kevin and head back to the States for treatment as an out-patient in Florida.

Back from treatment and back with Kai.

July 2001, with Mum, Kevin and Jordan at her birthday party in Planet Hollywood. I was loving being clean and loving being pregnant.

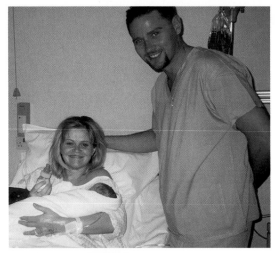

The birth of Jodie B, our little angel. Kevin looks great, I look a bit on the exhausted side.

Me and my beloved nan.

Walking back down the aisle a married woman, with my gorgeous husband.

On our honey-
moon and one
year clean!

The sexiest man in the
world and me, still
loving that Burberry!

Pre-op . . . the full extent of the
devastation to my nose.

Post-op . . . still a bit ape-like
because of the swelling. It was worth
all the pain to look normal again.

Publicity shot for *I'm a Celebrity, Get Me Out of Here*! On this occasion the snake wasn't real . . .

On a shoot with Mrs Lovely, aka super-stylist Marie, and Jeany Savage.

Leaving the jungle in 2003, with nothing left to prove. It was totally liberating.

On holiday in Antibes with the two men I owe my life to, my hubby Kevin and my minder Luc.

Me and my boy. Kai was my lifeline during the darkest days.

Me, my brothers Jay and Justin, Daddy and my little sister Georgia – the Westbrook clan. He doesn't look too bad considering how much hard work we are.

A family holiday to Disneyland, Paris in 2003, with Kevin, Jodie, Kai, Luc and our very own Mary Poppins, Sue Seale. This is what happiness means to me.

was pleased that I had finally found someone steady and strong to spend my life with. He had made an impression on my mother too. She liked the way he was with Kai, and she believed that he was the one man who was capable of helping me through my problems. But as well as we got on now, neither of my parents was keen to take me in. My father had a new partner and they had a daughter together, so there was no question that I could go and live with him permanently. And as far as my mother was concerned it simply wasn't an option. She didn't mind me staying for a while, but she knew that if I was going to get better then I had to stand on my own two feet. She had been to counselling to learn how deal with my addiction, and the first thing she had been taught was that she had to operate a system of tough love with me. If she kept giving in to me, if she kept allowing me to walk over her, then I would never improve. She promised to look after me and give Kai and me what we needed to live on, but she wasn't going to open the coffers and allow me access to what savings I had left because she knew that I would just end up spending it on drugs. The fact that ever since I'd first started working Mum had controlled my finances was a godsend, although it didn't feel like it at the time.

So in September 2000, completely broke, Kai and I moved into the room above the social club in South London. It was all I could afford. When I think back to that attic room with its foul-smelling, manky old furniture, its communal bathroom and filthy kitchen area, I am surprised we lasted there as long as we did. It was quite a comedown from anything I had ever known, as I had always lived in nice houses. Whether it was my parents' homes in Loughton, the first few flats I invested in, or the properties I shared with Kevin, they had all been lovely, and now I was down to this. It was humiliating.

When we first got together and I stopped working, Kevin had been happy to support me and Kai, but now we were apart I couldn't ask him for money. He still supported me in one way, paying for my car and my mobile phone, but he really did those things so that I was able to look after Kai properly, and he certainly wasn't going to give me any cash because he knew what I would spend it on.

Mum was the same. At first she made sure I had a weekly allowance of about £100 to care for Kai, but once she realised that I was spending it on drugs she gave me little bits of money here and there to tide me over and would go grocery shopping with me instead. We would have terrible fights about this. I'd go to her house in the middle of the night and say that I needed money for petrol, but rather than give me the cash, which would have been the easiest thing to do given that this usually happened at two or three in the morning, the poor woman would drag herself from her bed, get dressed and make me follow her to a petrol station so she could fill the car up for me. On one occasion when she refused to give me any money I started smashing up her bedroom, breaking all the mirrors on her cupboard doors. When she still refused I got her by the neck as though I was going to strangle her, and had my brother Jay not intervened I probably would have had a good go at it too.

I still got money by doing the odd shoot with Jeanie, but I certainly wasn't getting the kind of fees I commanded at the height of my career. I was so desperate for cash that I would take any work she gave me, no matter how tacky it was, and I'd always ask her to arrange for me to be paid up front.

So given my financial position I didn't have much choice but to take the room above the social club. It was squalid and it was rough, and the woman who ran it also had a nice sideline in drug dealing which didn't exactly help to reduce the amount of coke I was taking. But for now it was to be our home.

Kai was three years old by this stage and wasn't at school yet, but we had our daily routine. I would wake at around 9.30 in the morning, get Kai up from the bed we shared and make him his breakfast in the communal kitchen. Then I'd run him a bath and while he was splashing around in it I would quickly nip into the kitchen and prepare my own breakfast. There was no toast and cereal for me – just a large cup of coffee and half a gram of coke, which I would take in one large line. That's how I started each day. Not a single line, not even two: I needed half a gram to get me going first thing, and I would carry on using for the rest of the day.

Once Kai was out of the bath and I had dressed him we would go back to the room and I would spend the rest of the morning watching television, whilst he played with his toys and books on the floor. Come lunchtime I'd make him something to eat and then we'd head downstairs to the club.

It was a dingy, smoke-filled room, with lots of dark brown wooden furniture and a small bar in the corner. It made the Queen Vic look like the Ritz. The regulars, a group of old men, would sit there drinking all day. I'd find myself a table, order a Smirnoff Ice and sit there on my own whilst Kai would run around. At four o'clock the strippers would arrive, and Kai and I would retreat to our room to watch children's television.

Children are acutely aware of their surroundings from an early age. They like the security of knowing where they are, of being at home and in their bedroom surrounded by all their toys, but I had managed to deprive my son of that. He had gone from living in a large family home, where he had his own bedroom, a large garden and a swimming pool, to this.

His bedroom was my bedroom, his house was a social club, his garden – and his playroom – a dingy old bar. But he never complained, he never whinged; just so long as he was with me he was OK.

All through the day and night I would use cocaine.

I managed to give Kai a routine of sorts, but I didn't have one of my own. I only ate when I had to and only slept when I was capable of it. It was quite normal for me to stay up three nights in a row without any sleep. I'd take line after line until the dawn came up, and once it had I'd start all over again. I'd just carry on and on until I could no longer physically take any more.

There was nothing new in this. I had many sleepless nights in my early twenties after all. I vividly remember one morning back in the days when I was living in Buckhurst Hill, sitting in my flat watching television when *This Morning* with Richard and Judy started. I was on the sofa taking my gear and smoking with the curtains closed, thinking to myself that's odd, I'm sure that was just on. And then it dawned on me that I had actually been there in front of the television for a full 24 hours without even noticing, and the show had come back on again.

But now that I was at the social club these three-day binges happened much more frequently, sometimes as often as once a week. It wasn't long before I started suffering from blackouts and fits. I would suddenly just keel over, as though I had fainted, and whilst I was out my body would convulse and shake, as though I was an epileptic. When one of these happened I would wake to find Kai standing next to me, trying to shake me back to consciousness, putting sweets in my mouth and trying to give me his juice.

'I'll look after you, Mummy,' he'd say. 'I'll look after you.'

Kai was still so little, and he was very baby-like to look at with his round cherub face, chubby cheeks and big eyes, but he was actually very grown-up for his age. He could hold a proper conversation with you back then and was always asking questions about everything. I suppose this was probably to do with the fact that he spent most of his time surrounded by adults and didn't really socialise with any children his own age. So it must have been tough for him to see his mother like that. He didn't, of course, know that I was on drugs. He wouldn't have understood – although he knows now. And the one concession I made, in a vain attempt to be a good mother, was never to use them in front of him no matter how desperate I was for a fix. That was my rule. But he must have been disturbed by my behaviour, my highs and lows, my fits and black-outs, and that is the one thing above everything else that I will never be able to forgive myself for.

People often ask me now how I was able to afford all those drugs during that time if I was so broke. The answer to that is simple. I couldn't, but it wasn't a problem. You see, when you are the best-known drug addict in the country, you don't have to have the cash on you to get drugs when you want them. There is a system in that world called bail, which means that your dealer will bail you out with the cost of the drugs, and you pay him or her back at a later date. The last thing a dealer wants, after all, is for the addict to become clean simply because they can't afford it, and so they operate this handy credit system.

Because of who I was, people assumed that I would always be good for the money. They thought being famous, even if it was for all the wrong reasons by then, equalled being rich. It didn't help either, of course, that every time Kevin was mentioned in the press he was referred to as my 'millionaire boy-friend'. The fact was that although I still had the car Kevin gave me when we got engaged, a Porsche Boxter, I didn't own anything else of value. And I wasn't about to sell the car – I depended on it to get hold of my drugs. All my spending money, and there wasn't much, came from Mum or Kevin. No one really believed that I didn't have any money left though; they thought, they knew, that I would be able to get my hands on it eventually. And for a time they were right. If I suddenly got a modelling job or a royalty cheque from *EastEnders* then I would make sure the first thing I did with that money was pay off a debt. Rather than put the two or three grand cheque down on a deposit for a nice flat for us, I'd pay my dealer. And once I had settled that account I'd be good for some more. I worked this system with four of five dealers across London, paying them off in turn so that I was always good for credit with at least one or two of them at a time. But after a while, as with any debt, it escalated beyond my means and I was no longer in control of the situation. When this happened you had to brace yourself for a knock on the door and you would be threatened, often physically, until you paid it off. When my drug debts got out of control I would have to beg my parents or Kevin to help me out, and as loath as they were to do so I didn't give them much choice. They were so worried about what would happen to Kai if I didn't pay up, or what I would resort to in order to get my hands on the money, that they would find the money for me.

When I couldn't get bail easily I'd go downstairs to the club and work behind the bar. It was humiliating and the regulars would laugh out loud at me. I had gone from being a highly paid television actress to this, and they loved every minute of it. When I couldn't bring myself to do that I would spend what cash I had for Kai's groceries on drugs and then shoplift food for him. Pints of milk, tins of spaghetti – I became quite a dab hand at it. I even stole his birthday presents from a toy shop that year.

By the winter of 2000 I decided that we could no longer go on living like this, in such squalor. Perhaps it was what I deserved, being nothing more than a low-life junkie, but it wasn't right for Kai. I rang Social Services and asked if they could find us some better accommodation, but they refused on the grounds that they didn't believe that I didn't have any money. When, after about six phone calls and three meetings,

I managed to convince them that I didn't, they found us a room in a hostel. I had hoped that they would find us a council flat, but there was a long waiting list and so we were put up in a half-way house in Ilford. Frankly, had it not been for the fact that I had Kai I don't think they would have bothered.

I still had to pay rent, but it was subsidised. It was only £18 a night, but that was a lot to me, especially when you consider that a week's rent could buy you just over two grams.

The place was horrific, filled with truckers who bedded down there when they were on jobs, contract road workers and prostitutes, who you could hear going about their business throughout the night. We were given this tiny room with a carpet that was so filthy and sticky that you could not walk on it in bare feet. In one corner of the room was a bed, in another was a basin, and the bathrooms were communal. The only luxuries were the telly, fixed to the wall, and a kettle. There were no laundry facilities at the hostel, so every night I would have to wash Kai's clothes in the sink and then dry them with my hairdryer. There was no kitchen area but a canteen at the bottom of the hostel where you ate with the other residents. I tried to keep away from them, because I was worried that someone might recognise me and my secret would be out, but no one did. I am not sure why I worried. I had let myself go so badly by then that there were many days when if I caught my reflection in a shop window I didn't even recognise myself. So there was no reason why anyone should mistake me for the pretty little actress I once had been.

But the worst thing about this place was the fact that you couldn't stay there during the day. After breakfast that was it – you had to be out until it got dark. It was an extremely cold winter that year and I didn't know what we were going to do all day. Eventually I found a friend who lived round the corner and for a while we would spend the day at her house taking drugs till it was time to go back. In the end Kai and I only lasted there three weeks. I just couldn't take it any more, and so I packed our bags and we moved back to the social club.

It was hard for my family to watch me go through this period in my life, but they really didn't have much choice in the matter. Despite their constant pleas for me to return to rehab I wouldn't. I preferred to live like that than get clean. So, other than have me sectioned, which would have meant me losing custody of Kai, probably for ever, there was nothing they could do. The few times that my parents had taken me in I had behaved very badly, using their money for drugs, upsetting them, fighting with them and being generally abusive. They had got to the point where they just thought they could no longer help me, and that broke their hearts. My father would meet up with me because he wanted to see Kai, but he found it hard. He couldn't get over what I had become, what I had done to my looks and my life. I had it all at one stage. Now I'd lost it.

It was very tough on my mother because she couldn't escape the situation. Because I was financially dependent on her I saw more of her then than my father. I was either on at her demanding things, or I'd go for days with no contact at all. She couldn't decide which was worse. She would lie in bed at night waiting for someone to call and say that I was dead. If someone rang the doorbell she would think it was the police coming to tell her the news.

My mother thought she was exerting a regime of tough love, but it was always much tougher for her than it was for me. She didn't want to turn her back on me. She wanted me home, where she could look after me and love me, but she couldn't do it.

But the greatest tragedy of all for her was having to watch Kai, her only grandchild, go through all this too. She didn't want him to live like that, growing up surrounded by junkies, but she was helpless. She knew how much I loved Kai and that he was really the only thing in my life that was keeping me going. If I didn't have him, if I didn't have to care for him, who knew what would happen. I would probably give up and die from an overdose.

There were many times when she thought of taking him in for me, but she couldn't. Although Kai didn't have much of a relationship with his father then and never really saw him, he was in still in the picture. It would be very likely, if I gave up custody of Kai, that a court would send him to live with his father, as my mother had no legal rights. It was the same with Kevin. He had acted as a father to Kai when we had been together and loved him like his own son, and there were times when he wanted the boy to come and live with him, but again he had no rights as far as Kai was concerned.

All my parents and Kevin could do was to try and see him as often as they could, which they did. They would take him from the social club and spend the day with him at their homes. They would take him out for walks and to the playground, play with him in their gardens, make him something nice for tea, read him stories and buy him little presents. And I know now that as much as I loved Kai, and he loved me, during that time those days with Kevin away from the club, away from my drug taking, must have been the happiest of his young life.

14

MY LIFELINE

....

My mother was right. Kai was my lifeline and I truly believe that had he not come into my world I would probably be dead by now. He was the one thing in my life, outside of drugs, that really gave me pleasure and happiness. When all else had gone I still had Kai, he was my reason to live, to carry on. I am not going to say I was a good mother because I wasn't. I was awful. I put that poor little boy through so much during those years: I deprived him of a loving and secure home, of a normal family life, of his early childhood. But whilst I may not have been a good parent, that didn't mean I didn't love my child. I did. I loved him with all my heart and couldn't imagine my life without him. Whatever happened we would stick together. I had made that pact with Kai on the day he was born and I was going to stick to it.

Kai was such a good child. Despite what I put him through he never cried, he never whinged, and he never once complained. He just got on with it. Sometimes when I was very low and felt a bit tearful he would come up to me and ask me if I was OK.

'Are you sad, Mummy?'

'No, I'm not sad, Kai,' I'd say. 'I'm just a little tired, that's all.'

And he would pick up the toy he had just been playing with and come and sit very close to me. 'You can play this with me, Mummy,' he would say, looking up at me. 'That will make you happy.'

And the funny thing was that it did, every time. There is nothing more humanising, more humbling, when you are feeling like that, than to be in the presence of a child.

Kai wasn't spoilt in any way. Materially, of course, I couldn't have spoilt him as things were. Whilst we never went short of food or the real essentials – Kevin saw to that – there was no money for luxuries. He had a couple of toys, World Wrestling figures were his favourite at that age and I always made sure he had nice clothes. My parents gave him things when they saw him, and Kevin would always treat him to something really special on his birthday or sometimes just for the sake of it. But unlike a lot of other children Kai never asked for anything, not even when we were out at the shops.

He wasn't spoilt in terms of his temperament either. Given the way I behaved he could have had his moments, he would been entitled to them. He could have stamped his foot, raised his voice, demanded my attention, but he never did. There were never any hysterics, hissy fits or temper tantrums – not even as a toddler. He was just a very sweet-natured little boy.

I never let Kai out of my sight, and he was always by my side. That wasn't enough, however, for whilst I may have been physically there for my child, often I wasn't there in mind or spirit. No one who takes drugs can possibly claim to be a good parent. So long as you are using it isn't possible, because you can never give your child one hundred per cent of your attention. Even if you vow, like I did, not to use drugs in front of them, it isn't good enough because you are still high round them, still hung over the next day, and children pick up on these things even if they don't really understand them.

I knew that I was doing wrong by my son, and I felt guilty about that, and so I'd over-compensate by showering him with love and affection. I was always picking him up to kiss him, always hugging and cuddling him. Whilst I had been unable to give up drugs for Kevin, there were times when I convinced myself that I could do it for Kai. He was my child, my baby – I had brought him into the world. I owed him that much, I thought.

I'd lie in bed at night, watching him sleep next to me, and say, 'I'm going to do it for you, Kai. I promise I'll do it for you.'

*   *   *

Kai may have been quite well adjusted given the circumstances, but sadly I am not able to say the same thing about myself. My prolonged cocaine use had a very damaging effect on my mental state. One of the greatest misconceptions about cocaine is that it has no long-term mind-altering side effects, unlike other drugs such as LSD, heroin, mushrooms or some of the stronger weeds. Nothing could be further from the truth. Cocaine abuse can cause very serious psychological problems ranging from depression to psychosis and paranoid schizophrenia.

Even when I was just using the drug recreationally in my teens, cocaine had an effect on my personality. When I was on a high I lost all sense of what was going on around me. When I came down I was low and unhappy. When I was tired or hung over I was short-tempered and aggressive. By my early twenties I, like other addicts, had become consummate in the art of lying because I was desperate to conceal my problem; by my mid twenties I was shoplifting for food.

By the age of twenty-six, after seven years of extreme drug abuse, my head was not in a good place. Paranoia was beginning to eat away like a parasite at any sense of reason I had left. If someone so much as looked at me when I was walking down the street, which they often did because I was behaving so erratically, I would think that they were out to get me. If a car turned up outside the social club I'd assume it had come to take me away. I believed that there were people out there who wanted to hurt me, perhaps shoot me, or wanted me dead, and when I felt like that I'd hide away with Kai in our room. Because we had no curtains I would create a makeshift blind out of a blanket and put tape round the doorway so no one could see in. If I thought someone was coming I would turn the television off and all the lights out and sit there in silence until I was sure that they had gone away. If I heard someone on the stairs I would quickly rush to the bathroom and flush all my drugs down the loo. Then, twenty minutes later, when I was coming down, I'd realise that I had no gear left and would have to make a call . . . On and on it went.

Because I didn't like certain dealers to know where I lived, often I would go out to score. It didn't matter what time of day or night it was, if I needed drugs then I would have to have them there and then. I wasn't going to wait until the morning. If Kai was asleep I would wrap him in a blanket, carry him downstairs and put him in the car, and then I'd drive to some council estate where I would be met by a dealer. I'd get him to wrap the supply in cellophane so I could drive home with it in my mouth. That way, if I got pulled over by the police, I could swallow it. I only had to see a squad car in my rear-view mirror for that to happen and, when it did, of course, well then I'd be flying.

It was around this time that hallucinations began to set in. I would see rats and bugs crawling all over the floor and I'd scoop Kai up and we'd stay on the bed until they had gone. On one occasion I even managed to convince myself that there was a large black panther in our room. Quite what it was doing there, in a bedroom above a social club in South London, wasn't really clear. I was beyond any kind of rational thought by then. I would hear voices in my head, too. Sometimes they spoke to me directly, sometimes they would talk about me together. When that happened I would hold my breath in order to hear what they were saying, or if it got too much I'd turn up the volume on the TV to drown them out.

By now cocaine had made me psychotic. Not only had I smashed up my mother's bedroom and tried to strangle her when she refused to give me money for drugs; on another occasion I tried to crash the car I was driving her in, after we had been out for lunch one day. During the journey she had said something which I took completely the wrong way, so I sent the car into a spin. She started screaming at me to stop, calling me a maniac. And I just kept spinning the car, shouting 'I'm going to kill you, I am going to fucking kill you. You're a bitch and I hate you!' Fortunately, she somehow managed to get control of the wheel. Another time I drove my car at the window of a pub that Kevin owned, simply because he hadn't returned my call. When I failed to crash into it properly, I got out of the car, found a brick on the pavement and used that to smash the windows.

Although we had broken up we were still on speaking terms. Kevin didn't want to see me but he was worried about what I would do to myself if I had no contact with him at all. Often our conversations were very friendly and loving, and if I called him when I was low he would sit there for hours talking me through my problems. But when I had used too much and was in a dark mood I would call him at all times of the day and night and scream abuse at him. If he refused to take my calls and switched his mobile off then I would start sending him offensive text messages. My record was over fifty in one night. One evening when I thought he was avoiding me I rang him from the Porsche. I had Kai with me and had driven to Limehouse, in the Docklands.

When he answered the phone I said to him very coolly, 'I'm going to kill myself.'

'What did you say?'

'You heard. I'm going to kill myself. I've been to the chemist and bought loads of stuff. Enough for me and for Kai, too. I'm going to kill us both. I'm going to take all this medicine and go to Epping Forest and lie down and go to sleep with him.'

'Where the hell are you?' he shouted.

'I'm not telling you. You're not going to stop me. I mean it. I'm going to kill us both and there's nothing you can do about it.'

Kevin, of course, got it out of me in the end. It wasn't that difficult because I wanted him to find us, I wanted to see him. I had no intention of killing myself or Kai, I just wanted the attention. Kevin drove to the Docklands, found us and took us home. He took the Porsche off me that night.

'You're not driving that car any more. You're too ill, too out of your head. You're going to kill yourself, you can't be trusted with it,' he said.

The next day he gave me a new car, a little hatchback, with a tracking device attached to it. 'It's not for you,' he said when he showed it to me. 'It's for Kai. I need to know where he is at all times. I need to know he's all right.'

As well as the psychosis I frequently suffered from severe bouts of depression, which would hit me like a tidal wave, and could last for weeks on end. These got more and more severe until some days it was so bad that I didn't want to move from my bed, and had it not been for Kai I wouldn't have bothered. I would have lain there all day, curled up in a ball, if I hadn't had to look after him. I was constantly exhausted and didn't have the will or energy to do anything. I would just sit in my room staring at the television for hours on end, not taking any of it in. Completing the most basic daily task, such as brushing my hair or washing my face, became a huge ordeal during these times. I felt like I was just shutting down.

At night I would lie in bed crying into my pillow so Kai couldn't hear me. 'How did I get here?' I'd ask myself again and again. 'I had a lovely house, a loving family, a job, a man. And now I'm here in this grotty place, all alone, with no one.' I felt so isolated, so terribly alone in the world. And then I would think of my friends and wonder what my old Loughton friends like Ginnie and co were up to now. What they were doing with their lives. And I'd think: 'I bet they're happy, I bet they don't feel like this.' And then I'd turn my thoughts to the wonderful people I had met through work and how I had let them all down. I'd think of Sid, Barbara, Mike and Martine, of the friends I had made from the crew. What friends did I have now? What had happened to all those people I used to go out with at night? All the people I had given money to, taken out, bought drinks and drugs for – where were they now? And I'd just lie there silently sobbing my eyes out, until eventually, through sheer exhaustion, I had cried myself to sleep.

In the evening when Kai had gone to bed I'd sit on the floor and write letters and poems to him. I'd tell him how much I loved him, would apologise for being a bad mother, and try to explain why my relationship with his father hadn't worked out. In one letter I described how I felt the moment he came into the world, in another I talked about my own childhood. There were reams of these ramblings. Little verses written on the back of notepaper, pages and pages of thoughts written in biro and pencil on sheets of narrow-rule A4. I think I wanted him to know as much as possible about our life together in case anything happened to me. I wanted him to know that whatever happened I had always loved him and always would. But as much as these scribblings were for Kai, they were for me as well. I didn't really have anyone to talk to at this stage. My family and Kevin were at the end of the telephone, but there was only so much they could take, they had to get on with their own lives. So writing these letters and diaries was really a way of having a conversation with myself. It was like having a friend to talk to.

At the end of each letter to Kai I would always sign off promising to try and get better for him. I had tried to get clean for Kevin, the love of my life, but that hadn't worked. I had to do better by my son, I thought. I had to do it for him. He was dependent on me. I would vow to try to get clean, and when I went to bed that night I believed that I would. I'd think: 'I'm never going to touch it again. I'm never going to use. From tomorrow it's a new beginning.'

But, sure as clockwork, come eleven in the morning I was back on the stuff and I'd sit there with my cup of coffee and bowl of coke and think; 'I'm all right, I was just being stupid last night, that's all.'

And I would be fine for the rest of the day, but come the evening, as darkness fell, I was back to square one, feeling utterly miserable and helpless. It was a spiral from which I just couldn't seem to extract myself.

There were times when I felt suicidal. What did I have to live for, after all? I'd lost the love of my life, ruined my career, my looks, my health. Yes, I had brought it all on myself but that didn't make me feel any better about it – it just made me feel worse. I'd look in the mirror and feel disgusted at myself, at what I had done to my life, to my parents and my brothers, to Kevin and Kai. I couldn't see a way out, I couldn't imagine that I had a future. I'd look at Kai and think to myself that he would be better off without me. At least if I was out of the picture then he would have a chance of some happiness in life. He could start again. He was young enough. Just because I didn't have a future didn't mean that I had to deprive him of one as well. I'd lie in bed contemplating how I was going to do it. Maybe I would crash my car, maybe I would overdose. Sometimes I found myself in the chemist buying pills, planning to wash them down that night with a heady cocktail of alcohol and cocaine once I had taken Kai to my mother's for the evening.

But as strong as these feelings were to me at the time I don't think I ever really wanted to kill myself. I wasn't serious about it, otherwise I would have gone through with it. It was my own silent cry in the dark.

In the end, in total desperation and driven by guilt I took drastic action. It wasn't easy for me to make the call to Social Services. I loved my son and I didn't want to lose him. I didn't want him to be taken from me and put into care. I couldn't imagine waking in the morning and him not lying in the bed by my side, not chatting away to me during the day, not kissing me goodnight or flinging his little arms round me when he wanted a cuddle. Kai was my reason for living, but because of this very fact, I knew that he had to go and stay with someone else for a bit, while I sorted out my life. If I carried on like this I wouldn't be around for him, and that just wasn't fair. I had to make a go of things for him. I just couldn't give up like that. I had to try for his sake, as well as mine.

People ask me now why I didn't simply call my mother and have him stay with her while I went into recovery, but I knew that just wouldn't work. I had to do this myself, I had to put myself into a position where I would want to fight hard to get well. I knew that if Kai was with Mum, then I wouldn't really take our separation seriously. Before I knew it I would be back on the gear again, treating the break from my son as an extended holiday.

It was an extremely difficult decision for me to come to. No mother wants to put their child into care, but then again I wasn't like most mothers: I was a cocaine addict and I needed to get well. I wasn't doing it because I didn't love my child, I was doing it because I really did. On the occasions when either my mother or father had looked after Kai in the past I had never managed to stay clean, in fact I just took more drugs. If I was going to do it this time I knew I needed the right incentive. I would need to take a reality check, even if it was that extreme.

And so I picked up the phone and made the call to the relevant department. I didn't feel particularly proud doing it. It was, I can safely say, the worst call I have ever had to make in my life, but I didn't see that I had any choice in the matter. In the greater scheme of things what was worse for Kai? A couple of weeks away from his mother with a family who would love and care for him while I got better, or a lifetime without me? Because that is where I was heading.

At first the woman at the end of the telephone could not have been more helpful. She listened patiently as I went through my addiction history and explained how bad it had become. I was extremely honest with her about everything, from the quantities of coke I took to my behaviour when I was on the drug. I explained why I wanted to stop – because I feared that it would end up killing me – and that I planned to get myself clean for the sake of my son. Throughout the conversation I remained calm and collected.

Having heard my shameful tale she agreed that it would benefit Kai to go into care for a couple of weeks and said that given the situation she thought he was more than eligible to be put in the system. She said that she would put him with a kind and loving family until I got well enough to take him home again. All she needed was some details.

We started going through the questionnaire but only got as far as my name. The moment she discovered who I was she refused to help.

'You must be in a position to pay for someone to care for your son,' she said indignantly.

'I'm afraid I'm not.'

'I don't believe you.'

'Well, if I was, then I wouldn't be calling you for help.'

'We only help people who can't afford to help themselves, that's how it works. You are just not eligible, it's as simple as that. We can't help you.' And with that she put down the phone.

15

ONE LAST CHANCE

....

One small step forward, one giant leap back, that was how it felt at the time. My decision to put Kai into care hadn't been taken lightly. I wasn't copping out, shirking responsibility for my child or trying to pass him on to someone else because I no longer wanted him. I didn't want to lose him, I just wanted things to work out. It was by no means the easy option. I had made that call because I had to, because I was trying to save my life and make a new and better one for my son. But the reaction I had from Social Services was like a slap in the face. For the first time in my life I was trying to do something constructive about my problems, I was trying to do something for my son.

Maybe I had gone about it the wrong way. Maybe it wasn't the right option. Or maybe she was right and I didn't deserve any help. But what upset me most about that conversation was that until she knew who I was she had agreed that my chosen course of action was the appropriate one and that it would be best for us both in the long run. Was I to be penalised in this way just because I had once been on television? Was no one going to take me seriously because I had been famous? Did all that come before the welfare of my child? It wasn't as though someone else had called to ask them to intervene. I had done it myself. It had been a brave move. One I had only made because I really needed help and had thought they were there to give it to me.

I was angry, really angry. The fact that I had once been a highly paid actress meant nothing to Kai. It was not his reality. He wasn't the son of a famous soap star, he was the son of a young, unemployed woman, who had no money, who was severely addicted to cocaine and badly needed some help. But on hearing my name they had simply closed that door to him.

I had so wanted to get better then, but I just couldn't cope with what had happened. I had made the first tentative step in my mission to get clean, but when I was knocked back like that I took it very badly. I took it personally. 'OK, don't help me, that's fine,' I thought. 'But what about my son? What did he do to be rejected by you?' The hardest step for anyone to make in their recovery is the first one. I had managed it by admitting for the first time in my life that I had a problem.

I was so vulnerable after that. Any wind I had in my sails seemed to have gone for good. I felt flat and helpless and I couldn't see a way out of my problems.

And when that happens to someone in my position, what do they do? They turn to the one thing they know will see them through that moment. Wine, whisky, vodka, gin, painkillers, uppers, downers, weed or smack – you just have to name your poison. For me that was coke, and within minutes of making that call I'd made another to my dealer. Well, why not? I thought. I might as well, since no one cared whether I got clean or not.

I carried on using cocaine heavily for a couple of weeks just to try and anaesthetise the pain, but after a while, even through the numbness, I realised that it was crazy. I am not going to pretend I stopped using, because I didn't, but I realised that I had to get my life back on track. I could no longer carry on living this life – I wasn't even living, I was just existing – so I decided to do something about it for once. My life was so empty. There was nothing good or happy about it. I had nothing to look forward to and it dawned on me that as Kai grew up he would come to realise what his mother really was. I had to make a change.

My first step was to try to sort out what was left of my career. At the beginning of 2001, on the advice of a friend in the industry, I decided to change my agent and enlisted the services of a woman called Cheryl Barrymore. To the outside world Cheryl was perhaps better known as the former wife of the popular light entertainment presenter and comedian Michael

Barrymore, but within the industry she had made a name for herself as a respected manager. From our first meeting we hit it off and I knew that she was going to be the right person to look after me. What was wonderful about Cheryl was that she never once judged me. She knew all about what it was like to be a cocaine addict, having been married to one. Over the years Michael had his own very public battle with the drug and she had tried for a time, until their marriage came to an end, to help him through it. She understood that the drug was rife on the celebrity circuit; she knew from first-hand experience what it did to people, how it affected them; and, most important of all, she understood that addiction is a disease. She didn't believe that people should be hung out to dry because they couldn't stop themselves from using, or left out in the cold because they took an illegal substance. She thought people should be allowed to rebuild their lives and start again.

When I told her this was what I wanted she agreed to take me on and said that she would support me not just professionally but emotionally as well. I realised how lucky I was to have met her, and she quickly became a good friend of mine. Kai and I would spend hours at her house playing with her little dog Gucci, eating dinner with her and talking through my problems. She encouraged me to get on top of my career again, to work things out with Kevin and, whatever happened, to make a stable home for Kai.

But one of the most amazing things Cheryl did for me was to encourage me to see a therapist called Beechy Colclough, who had treated Michael in the past. Beechy had worked with a lot of famous people with addiction problems over the years and he had an incredible reputation. When the photograph of me leaving the Soap Awards had been published the year before, Sir Elton John, who fought his own successful battle with cocaine addiction, had been quoted in the papers as saying that Beechy was the one person who could help me. I hadn't done anything about it at the time, because I didn't really want to get clean, but now I had Cheryl acting not only as my agent but as my mentor as well. She knew I wasn't going to get clean overnight, I was too bad for that, and she also understood that I would only come off drugs when *I* wanted to. She knew, from her experiences with Michael, that it was not enough for other people to want me to get clean – I had to come to that decision myself – but she hoped that my one-to-one sessions with Beechy might help me come to that conclusion eventually.

I had never seen the point of therapy before. During my stints in the Priory and the Nightingale I had countless sessions, but they never did anything for me. When I was in group therapy I would just switch off and go into my own little world whilst the other addicts recounted their life stories. In one-to-one sessions I would get defensive with the therapist, and often snap back when I was asked a question, or I'd sit there in silence refusing to speak. But with Beechy it was very different. Here was this very mild-mannered, softly spoken man who wanted to get to know me. He didn't just talk to me as an addict, he spoke to me as though I was a human being. It was very refreshing. He knew that I was still using. He didn't expect me to give up after one session with him. And there were times when I'd arrive at his office and be completely out of it, and then he would make me sit down and discuss how I was feeling and what had driven me to get to that position. I found it very helpful and began to see that maybe I did have a life outside of drugs.

For a while everything in my life seemed to be going well. Not only did I have a new agent, a therapist I liked and trusted, but I had also got back together with Kevin. When he knew that I was trying to get my life back on track he invited me and Kai to come and live with him once again, and so we moved out of the social club. Kevin hadn't split with me because he didn't love me, he broke up with me because he couldn't live with me as a drug addict. The fact that I was now getting my life back together and was making an effort to get clean meant a lot to him. He said he would stand by me and help me through it.

With my man back at my side again I decided to turn over a new leaf, determined that we should make a go of it. I started making an effort with my appearance again, having my hair cut and highlighted. My mother was also cautiously pleased that I was trying to get clean, and following assurances that I would not spend any money on drugs she even allowed me access to some money from my savings, so at last I was able to buy some nice clothes. I even managed to cut down on my drugs intake. And so for a time everything looked rosy again. I had my man, my son, a home, a life and a career, and to top it all I discovered I was pregnant. It hadn't been planned as such, but Kevin was just over the moon. We both were.

But once again my happiness was to be short-lived. I am not sure what drove me to it − I had, after all, got everything I wanted in life − but within just a couple of months of Kevin and me being together again I was back to my old ways once more. The fact that I was pregnant didn't stop me; nor did the fact that I had been told that I was lucky that Kai was so healthy given that I had taken drugs throughout the time I was expecting him.

I was using heavily again. There is something innately arrogant and selfish about the addictive personality that makes you feel and act as though you are above and beyond normal codes of behaviour. I should have been thankful for the fact that my fiancé had given me a second chance. I should have been happy not only still to have Kai but another child on the way. I should have respected the fact that Cheryl was going out of her way to take me on. But I didn't. After a while I just took it all for granted and stupidly began taking large quantities of the drug again.

I suppose I thought I could get away with it, that no one would notice. They did, however, and the first person to do so was Kevin. He was furious. He felt betrayed and used and hurt that I could put the health of our baby at risk. Once again we broke up and I went to stay with a friend for a couple of weeks before moving into a flat in the Docklands. As I started taking more of the drug I began to behave psychotically again. When he refused to take my call one morning, I rang his PA at his office and booked one of his cars, in my name, to take me to an abortion clinic. Of course I had no intention of even setting foot in the clinic, but I knew that it would break his heart if he thought that I had. After four hours of hiding out in the area I rang his office again and left a message with the receptionist, knowing she knew where I had gone.

'Can you tell Kevin, when he returns, that I have had an operation,' I said to her when she answered the phone. It wasn't enough that I wanted to hurt Kevin by letting him think I had aborted his child, I wanted to humiliate him too by making sure that everyone in his company knew about it. Eventually, after a couple of hours, I relented and let him know the truth.

I successfully managed to conceal my drug taking from Cheryl for a while. When I was very high on drugs I just kept away from her or didn't answer her calls. So, oblivious to what was going on, she started to get me some work. Although I was up for a couple of roles it was really just publicity work to start with.

It started with a prime-time television interview with Martin Bashir, the journalist who famously interviewed the Princess of Wales for *Panorama* and more recently Michael Jackson. It was followed by a couple of newspaper and magazine interviews and then a big spread in *OK!* magazine, where I posed with my little bump. In each interview I spoke about how great it was to be clean and off drugs and how the publication of the photograph of my missing colonna had shocked me into making a recovery. For a time I think the public bought my story, but in February of 2001 my drug taking was exposed again when I appeared on the live Channel 4 show *The Priory*.

I am not sure why Cheryl booked me on to the show. She was well aware by then that my drug taking was out of control. The morning I was due to appear on the programme I turned up at her house off my head, begging her not to let me on it.

'Please, Cheryl, I'm not well, tell them I can't do it.'

'It's too late, Danni, you'll just have to get yourself together.'

Rather than lay off the drugs that afternoon I was so nervous about going on the programme that I just kept taking coke through the day until I arrived at the studio.

It was a complete disaster right from the word go. When I was introduced onto the set by the show's presenters Jamie Theakston and Zoë Ball I could barely walk. When I sat down I couldn't focus and didn't understand their questions. I kept sipping water from a bottle because my mouth was so dry. When Zoë Ball asked me whether I was clean I told her I was and then said something about seeing Beechy, only I couldn't pronounce his name or explain who he was. They were exchanging knowing looks and started laughing at me. It was awful. Needless to say it was all over the papers the next day.

When I went to Cheryl's the following morning and watched the recording I just couldn't believe it. I knew it had gone badly but I didn't realise to what extent. It wasn't a car crash, it was a train crash. I sat there looking at myself, trying to get my head round the situation. I despised myself, and Cheryl knew it.

'Maybe this is what you needed to see, Danni,' she said to me as we sat on her sofa. 'Maybe now you'll realise how bad you are when you are out of it. Maybe now you might do something about it.'

I became very depressed and despondent over the next couple of weeks. I retreated into my own little world, unable to talk to or see anyone. My family, especially my grandmother, had been really distressed about the show and the publicity it generated. I couldn't face seeing Kevin, I was too ashamed. So the only people I had left to talk to were Beechy and Cheryl.

But I didn't help myself with either of them. Every time I saw them I was so high on coke that it was impossible for them to get through to me. After a while

Beechy said that he should stop seeing me, so now I only had Cheryl left.

Bored one afternoon, I decided to go and see her at her house in Stanhope Terrace. I wasn't feeling very well and I wanted to be with someone. I had Kai with me and thought that I could just spend a couple of hours with her while Kai played with Gucci. I had been up most of the night before using and hadn't had much sleep. I hadn't eaten for the best part of two days and had taken coke that morning. When Cheryl opened the door to me she gasped. She had seen me out of it before, but never this bad, I was all over the place. She escorted me into the house by the arm and sat me on the sofa. In the last few weeks I had lost a lot of weight and she couldn't get over how scrawny I looked. My skin was grey, almost translucent. My eyes kept rolling, unable to focus on anything. She called to her maid to ask her to make me a cup of sweet tea, hoping that it might make me feel a bit better, and went into the next room to call Kevin, but when she returned it was too late.

By the time Cheryl came back into the sitting-room I had slumped off the sofa and was lying on the floor, my body fitting in convulsions. Kai was standing over me.

'Mummy's ill,' he kept saying. 'Mummy's ill.' 'Wake up, Mummy.'

Cheryl tried to hold me down, in the way that you would with someone having an epileptic fit, to stop me from harming myself. She couldn't wake me up, she couldn't get me to open my eyes. My skin had gone green, my lips an eerie shade of blue.

I had overdosed.

Cheryl managed to reach for the phone and called my doctor. Dr Brenner specialises in drug addiction and had treated me at the Priory. He said he was on his way and told Cheryl what to do in the meantime. Within less than an hour he was there by my side, medicating me. It wasn't an easy thing to do because I was three months pregnant at the time, so there were certain things he couldn't give me, such as any drug containing methadone. Instead, once he had brought me round he gave me a gentle cocktail of sleeping pills, Valium and Mogodons. The idea was to knock me out so that my body could rest.

Doctor Brenner explained to Cheryl that if I carried on like this without receiving medical help then I would be dead in a fortnight. The fact was I was now so sick, so poisoned by the drugs, that all my organs were beginning to shut down. My liver and kidneys were no longer functioning properly and my heart rate was very low. As he treated me in her bedroom Cheryl hit the phone.

After calling Kevin, Mum and Beechy to put them in the picture she called my solicitor, because she was concerned about what would happen to Kai if I died. Jeremy Freedman had been my solicitor for the last eight years and was the most wonderful, trustworthy man. He had seen me through my divorce from my first husband and had helped sort out Kai's custody when his father and I broke up. He was very upset when Cheryl told him what had happened and said that he and his wife would take me to their home while I got better.

'You can't put your family through that,' Cheryl said. 'You don't know what an addict is like. She might be quiet like she is now, but come tomorrow she might be smashing the house down trying to get out, to get drugs.'

When Kevin arrived to collect Kai and take him to my mother's he talked to Cheryl and the doctor about what to do next. Doctor Brenner said that I had to go into treatment and I had to go quickly, otherwise I was going to die. They called Beechy, who was at home at the time, and he got on the phone and arranged for a place for me at the Cottonwood Drug Rehabilitation Unit, in Tucson, Arizona. It was a long way to go, but the clinic had one of the best reputations in the world and, unlike so many treatment centres in this country, at Cottonwood they would be able to give me the medical attention I needed. You see, a lot of clinics that deal with drug treatment only deal with mental side of addiction. They don't have the facilities or the medical doctors on hand to look at the physical problems your drug dependency might have caused.

There was just one problem: I wasn't yet well enough to fly.

In order to be in a fit state to make the journey I was going to have to undergo a detox. I had a lot of toxins in my body, and if I was to survive such a long plane journey they would first have to make sure that my organs were functioning. Another reason why I had to do the detox was that no airline would allow me on to a plane unless a doctor had given written certification that I was well enough to fly.

They discussed putting me into a detox programme in a hospital in London, but both Kevin and Cheryl were nervous about the press finding out about it. They didn't want me to be put under any more pressure, so it was agreed that I would do a two-week home detox under Dr Brenner's supervision.

I was fortunate that they had come to that decision. Coming off drugs, going through cold turkey, is not a pretty sight. It makes you very ill: not only are you incredibly sick for those first few hours but your mood swings can be violent. Despite all that I had done to him in the past, Kevin agreed that I should do it in my flat in the Docklands. As well as my visits from Dr Brenner, who came every two days, I would be looked after by Kevin's closest friend Luc Peeters and his wife Angela. He hired two minders to make sure I didn't run away and to deal with me if I got out of control. Kevin promised to visit me, but he knew that it wasn't good for me if he was around the whole time. And he was right.

One evening he came to see me and we were in my

bedroom on the ground floor, with a minder in the next room. Kevin had been with me for about half an hour when he told me he had to go.

I started screaming, 'You can't go, you can't, you can't leave me like this!'

'I have to,' he said. 'I'll come back later.'

But later wasn't good enough. I needed him there now. I lost it. I picked up the television from the sideboard, yanking the plug out of the wall, and threw it at him. I smashed my hand through the wall – it was only made of plywood but it still hurt – and was yelling at the top of my voice. Kevin called in the minder, who took hold of me and tried to calm me down.

We were in the hallway by now and Kevin was leaving by the front door.

'I've got to go, Danni, I'm so upset, I can't see you do this to yourself.'

When he had gone I ran into my room and slammed the door. I suppose the minder thought I had just gone in there to sulk or lick my wounds, so he left me to it. But as soon as the door closed I opened the window and climbed out. It was pouring with rain and I was barefoot and wearing only a nightdress. I ran on to the highway, dodging the traffic as I made my way into the middle of the road. I was lucky not to be run over by a bus, which fortunately swerved to avoid me.

Kevin was driving down the road when he saw me standing there, screaming and crying. I was hysterical.

I was soaked through, my nightdress clinging to me. He braked, nearly causing a pile-up, ran from the car and grabbed me. He took me back home, dried me and changed my clothes. He locked the window and stayed with me until I fell asleep.

He said it was one of the most difficult moments of his life. The next few days were hellish. I suffered from mood swings, sleepless nights, the sweats and was violently ill. I was terrified at the prospect of getting clean. But I had no choice: I had to go through with it, if I was going to live.

After a fortnight of detox Dr Brenner said I was fit to fly and wrote a letter certifying this, but finding an airline that would take me was still a problem. None of them wanted that responsibility. They all said no except for Virgin Atlantic. Once Dr Brenner had explained the gravity of the situation and told them that unless I went to Cottonwood I would probably die, they agreed. They were very understanding and said that they would do anything to help.

I don't think I really understood what was going on at that time. I remember the day before I flew to America saying to Cheryl that I needed to go to Selfridges and asking her to come with me.

'What on earth for?' she asked.

'I'll need some new clothes for when I'm out there. Some sun-glasses and I'd like a couple of bikinis too.'

'You're going to rehab, not a holiday resort!' she said.

I sighed. 'Don't you think a couple of days at Champney's would do it?'

'Danniella! You just don't get it, do you?'

It was decided that Luc would make the journey to Phoenix with me. It was too painful for Kevin. I was carrying his child, and had possibly just days to live. And if that wasn't upsetting enough for him, the poor man had only just lost his mother. I was in such a bad place mentally. I was so volatile around him – so fragile yet so psychotic. He couldn't do with the aggro, with me fighting him, and eventually with the pain of having to put me in there. He might have given in. He knew that it would be different with Luc. He knew I would listen to him and that he could stand up to me.

Weighing in at 23 stone, Luc could certainly handle me physically. It wasn't just a question of his size either. Luc worked out and trained every day. If anyone was going to be able to get me to America in one piece then it was him. He can be fierce but he is also a gentle giant and always has looked out for me. When I was going through the home detox, every time I woke he was there sitting on a chair, watching me, looking after me. I don't think he got a wink of sleep in that time.

Luc and I flew to Phoenix from Gatwick airport. Once we checked in I made my way to the bar. It was seven in the morning. Luc assumed I was getting a coffee but I returned with a vodka and cranberry juice. I still wasn't getting it. I remember having a row with Kevin on the phone because he wouldn't let me buy a pair of Gucci sun-glasses from Duty Free.

'But I need them,' I pleaded.

'No you don't. What you *need* is to go and get well, Danni!'

Much to my delight when I got on the plane I discovered that they had a credit card phone in the seat. Well, that was it, I was in heaven. I rang everyone I knew and abused them. I rang Kevin and shouted at him, then rang again and told him I was going to go and screw everybody I could in the treatment centre just to piss him off. I was a bitch. A month later he got a bill for £3,000 for the calls. £3,000 for an earful of abuse from the girl whose life he was trying to save.

We were in First Class, paid for by Kevin, of course. From the stash of medicines Dr Brenner had given him Luc gave me a couple of pills to calm me down and try to get me to sleep. But I didn't take them, and when Luc nodded off about four hours into the flight I climbed over him and headed for the loos.

I locked the door behind me and lit up a cigarette. When I came out there were three stewardesses waiting outside looking at me.

'What's your problem?' I sneered.

'Have you been smoking?' one asked.

'So what if I have?' I said. 'What you gonna do, open the door and chuck me off the plane?'

They went over to Luc, woke him up and said that they were going to have to shackle me to the seat and when we arrived in LA, where we were supposed to be meeting our flight to Arizona, have me deported.

'No, please don't, she's really ill, and she's going to die,' he pleaded.

I, in the meantime, was now standing on my seat shouting and swearing at all the stewardesses and passengers looking at me.

'What the fuck are you looking at, you stuck-up bastards? Wankers!' I made a horrible scene, shouting at these poor people.

Luc grabbed me and calmed me down and they agreed not to shackle me. At the other end they gave me a caution and said that they understood that I was ill, which was kind of them.

I was fine by that time and we got on a connecting plane to Phoenix. I slept the whole way. I guess I had just run out of steam by then.

We got to Arizona really late at night. This friendly old man met us at the airport and drove us for about an hour to the treatment centre. We got out of the car and they took my bags and ushered me into reception, but as I checked in a flash bulb went. There was a photographer standing there. He had followed us from England. The security guards tried to push him away, but he put his camera to the window of the lobby and took pictures of me.

They chased him off the grounds but couldn't find him because the centre was surrounded by desert and it was dark. But the pictures made the front pages of the tabloids back in Britain the next day.

Once they had checked me in, Luc turned to me and gave me a hug.

'I've got to go now, Gucci,' he said, using the pet name he had for me. I've got to leave you.'

'No, no, you can't go! Stay with me!'

'I can't. I'm not allowed.'

'Then take me with you, I can't stay here!'

And all I can remember after that is lying on the floor holding on to his leg like a two-year-old, begging him to take me with him. As he walked through the room, with me dragging along behind him screaming like a child, tears rolled down his face. When he reached the exit the staff picked me up from the floor, and as he waved goodbye to me they gave me an injection.

16
RECOVERY

....

I woke up the following day at around two in the afternoon feeling quite groggy. I opened one dry eye, then the next, and looked round the room, failing to see anything I recognised. I had no memory of the night before, no recollection of travelling to Arizona. I had no idea where I was. Everything in the room was a brilliant white: the walls, the bed, the sheets, the table next to me, the little gown I was wearing. As I adjusted myself on my pillows looking at my new surroundings I was blinded by this incredibly bright light shining through the net curtains that hung over the window. 'Oh my God!' I thought. 'That's it. I'm dead.'

Feeling confused and panicky I got out of bed and made my way to the window. My legs felt so heavy under me that I had to steady myself on the side of the bed frame to prevent them from buckling under me.

'Where am I, where am I?' I said to myself.

I had a dull pain at the front of my head.

I slowly made my way to the window and pulled back the curtain, and when I looked out I just couldn't believe my eyes. All I could see for miles and miles was just this never-ending sea of bright yellow sand, punctuated at intervals by giant cactus plants. I had never seen anything like it in my life. There was nothing on the horizon, no other building or house in sight. All there was . . . was sand. That was it.

As I stood there, still trying to get my head round where I was, I heard voices outside my room. I turned round, and through the glass in my door I could see a group of nurses at a station outside my room, standing there talking to one another in hushed tones. I made my way to the other side of the room, supporting myself with the furniture as I went along, and realised that there was another curtain sectioning off a window. I pulled it back. There was a long corridor, filled with nurses and other rooms.

I was on a ward.

I was in a hospital.

I opened the door and went to the nurse's station. 'Where am I?' I asked.

'You're at Cottonwood,' one of them replied in a soft Southern accent. 'Cottonwood, Arizona,' she added, obviously sensing my confusion.

And then I remembered. I remembered coming here; I remembered the friendly old man who met me at the airport and brought me here; I remembered being scared by the flash of the camera bulb as I checked in, and I remembered Luc leaving. And I realised then where I was. 'Oh God,' I thought. 'I have to get out of here, fast.' But how could I? This wasn't like the Nightingale. I couldn't just do a runner from here in the middle of the night, hailing a black cab on Marylebone High Street to take me home. I didn't know anyone in Arizona. I didn't have any money. I didn't know how you got a cab to come and collect you from the middle of the desert.

I timidly asked a nurse whether it might be possible for me to use the telephone.

'Of course,' she said, handing it to me over the desk, and then she discreetly moved away, to give me some space. I picked it up and, somewhat amazingly remembering to dial the international code for the UK, rang Kevin. It was the middle of the night in London.

'Kevin?' I said quietly.

'Danni,' came a sleepy and confused voice from the other end of the phone. 'Danni, is that you?'

'Yes, of course it's me! You bastard!' There was venom in my voice.

There was a pause from his end.

'Where the fucking hell have you left me?' I screamed. 'I'm in the middle of the fucking desert – what the fuck have you done to me? There's just a load of fucking sand out there! I'm not staying here. I'm coming home. Do you hear me? I am coming fucking home. So sort it out and while we're on the subject tell me where my fucking passport is!'

I lost it. I completely lost it. The nurses were staring at me, horrified by the behaviour of their latest charge.

Kevin knew he couldn't get into a fight with me. 'OK then,' he said merrily. 'Get well soon, I love you.'

'Well, I don't fucking love you!' I said at the top of my voice. 'Right now, I fucking hate you!' I shouted as I slammed down the phone.

It took me ten days to calm down.

Much to my horror I realised a couple of hours later that I had been confined to the nutter's room. OK, they didn't call it that exactly, but that's what it was. A room for the nutters and loons. I was on suicide watch, which is why I was in a windowed room next to the nurses' station. Every moment of the day I had to be watched. When they weren't coming in to bother me, to prod and poke me, and take tests from me, they were there, outside, peering through the window at me, taking notes. When I would wake in the night, they were there staring at me. When I came to in the morning they were there again. I felt like a fish in a tank. I hated it. I wanted to get out. Each day and night felt incredibly long. I had nothing to do other than talk to them, answer questions and take pills. I had no idea what drugs I was being given and for the first time in my life I rather perversely seemed to care what I was being fed. They would just arrive, these little pills, at intervals, in small paper cups. And as much as I protested I was forced to take them.

Because I had been so ill when I overdosed, much of the time during my first few days at the centre was spent seeing doctors. They monitored my heart rate and sent me off every few minutes, it seemed, for blood and urine samples. I was quite amazed by this and, if I am honest, secretly impressed. It was as though they were trying first to get my body well before they tackled my mind.

On my second day there a psychiatrist came to see me and explained that she had been assigned to me for the duration of my stay. She seemed incredibly severe and tough, and I found out later that you only got put with her if you were considered to be a difficult case. I wasn't sure I liked her, but that wasn't the point. She wasn't employed there to be my friend, she was there to sort my head out. She told me that if I needed to speak to someone while I was in the clinic then I only had to ask. There was a team of counsellors on hand round the clock to talk to the patients, so even if it was three in the morning, there would be someone there for me.

The next person to turn up in my room was the nutritionist, who weighed me, measured me and took some more tests. We talked about the diet I had been on – cocaine, booze, chocolate and fags; and we discussed the diet they would put me on at the clinic – fruit and vegetables, protein and dairy foods. I was three months pregnant, but I was so thin. The nutritionist wanted to get a lot of calcium and nutrients into my body quickly, not just to help my recovery but for the baby's sake as well.

After four days of being locked up in the nutter's room I was deemed sane enough to be moved on to a normal ward. I was put into a dormitory with eight other 'inmates', as I liked to think of us. Compared to the treatment centres I had known before, this one wasn't so bad. The bedrooms were bright and airy, and the bathrooms were nice too, but what I hadn't bargained for was that whilst I was staying here I would have to clean them. And not only that but I was going to have to make my bed, keep the room tidy and pick my clothes up off the floor. When I was told this I was outraged. It was costing a small fortune to keep me incarcerated in this dump as it was, so the least they could do was clean up after me. I sounded spoilt and I was. As an addict all I could ever do was think about myself and put myself first. I didn't realise that being self-reliant was just part of the treatment.

And so began the first stage of my recovery. Daily life in the clinic was regimental. I had never known anything like that in my whole life, not even when I had been at school. We would be woken at seven and then would have to form a queue in our pyjamas in the corridor and wait to be issued with our morning medication one by one. When you reached the head of the queue, you'd give the nurse your name and then you would be handed your morning meds, all in a little paper cup. It was like a scene from *One Flew Over the Cuckoo's Nest*.

You'd have to stand there with a plastic cup of water in one hand and the paper one filled with your pills in the other. Then you'd put them in your mouth and wash them down with a glug of water; but only when you'd opened your mouth again, wiggled your tongue around and stuck it out and lifted it up to prove to the nurses that you had swallowed your little helpers, were you free to go.

Once we had our meds we were allowed to return to our rooms and have a quick shower. Then we would get dressed, make our beds and head down to breakfast. Because there were a lot of people, both men and women, being treated for sex addiction in the clinic, we were not allowed to wear anything remotely revealing at the centre, not even a vest top, much to my distress. Our daily uniform consisted of baggy sweat pants and an oversized T-shirt. Even on the days that we were allowed to swim in the clinic's pool there was no question of squeezing oneself into a micro bikini. If you wanted to swim then you had to be in a swimsuit, and if you were hanging out by the pool they liked you to be dressed or covered by a towel.

If you were really lucky and made it on to the second stage of the programme you were allowed out at night. A minibus would pick a group up and take them into the local town, and this was a very big deal, believe me.

At the clinic we weren't allowed to listen to music, even if it was classical, so going into town and hearing music for the first time was magic to the ears. It was pure heaven, however bad the music was. In fact we were so restricted in the clinic that we were not even allowed to read books. We could look at literature about recovery, but that was it.

Shortly after breakfast we had our first 'home meeting'. We'd be split into different groups depending on how difficult you were, how nutty you were, how druggy you were, and you'd begin the day by talking about your issues in group therapy. The rest of it was spent following a curriculum of art therapy, serenity trails through the desert, medical checks, one-to-one counselling and an induction into the twelve-step programme. This was our day: wall-to-wall meetings, nothing else. Even in the evening after we had finished our supper we were encouraged to use our recreational time constructively and attend voluntary meetings. It was my idea of hell.

And if that wasn't bad enough we weren't allowed to smoke in the building or use our mobiles. Calls could be made, but only at certain times, and they were rationed.

All I wanted to do in those first few days was to get out of there, fly back to London and get back to normal.

All I wanted to do was take drugs again.

Every three days Kevin would send me flowers.

'I'm so proud of you, darling.' 'It will be worth it in the end.' 'Keep going, I love you.' I cared that Kevin was keeping in touch but I didn't want to keep going, it wasn't worth it, I couldn't give a damn if he was proud – all I wanted to do was to leave as soon as possible. When he called me I'd sit there on the phone and scream at him.

'Just get me out of here! I don't care what it costs, I can't stay here!'

'I hate you for doing this to me. I'm never going to talk to you again!'

'All I can see out of my fucking window is fucking sand and fucking cacti. There's not even a fucking shop round here! What the fuck am I supposed to do?'

And so it went on, for days and days. When I did have some rare time to myself I would sit on the small veranda outside my room, chain smoking. 'How did I get here?' I thought. 'What the hell am I doing in this loony bin?'

Although Kevin called me from time to time when I was allowed phone calls, and sent me flowers, I didn't have any other contact with anyone back home. My cousin's little girls did write me sweet letters saying how much they loved me and wanted me to get better, and drew me pictures, which I hung on my wall, but other than that I heard from no one else from my family during that time. I had no contact with Mum and Dad, which did upset me for a while.

But the one person I couldn't bear not hearing from and not being allowed to have any contact with was Kai. I missed him so much and longed to be with him again. You see, whatever was going to happen with Kevin in the future was up to us, that was for him and for me to work out, but it wasn't the same for Kai. He was my baby, who needed me and loved me. As far as anyone else was concerned I may have just been a helpless junkie, but to Kai I was simply his mother. I'd lie in bed at night stroking my new little bump, as tiny as it was because I was so thin, and think that's OK, we have each other here, but what about Kai, how is he coping with this?

I had assumed, from the moment I overdosed and Mum had taken care of Kai, that she would look after him while I was in treatment, and that was what we had agreed. It was the perfect solution and everyone was happy about it. Kai was used to staying with her and that made me happy because I had never been separated from my son for such a long stretch of time before. Mum and Dad had become close friends again, so he would be constantly popping round, and there were my brothers who adored their nephew and Kevin who was always welcome in my Mum's house. It seemed perfect for everyone involved, but sadly it didn't work out.

Social Services, having previously refused to take my situation seriously, having denied us access to a proper home when we had nowhere else to go, having prevented me from putting Kai into care when I initially wanted to get clean, suddenly decided to wade in at the last moment. They had seen my performance on *The Priory*, read the subsequent stories, pored over the pictures of me checking into the clinic, and from that moment decided that they should get involved in my case. Too much, too late, was all I could think when I heard the news later on.

Despite the fact that everyone was standing by me and helping me get through this ordeal, they decided to take action against me and declare me an unfit mother. Months before, *I* had declared myself unfit, I had actually asked for help – and they had refused it. Now that I was thousands of miles away from my son they stepped in. Kai was fine, he was safe, he was loved, and all he knew was that his Mummy had gone away for a little time to get better and that as soon as she was she would be back with him.

Now Kai had been moved from his grandmother to his father. When I heard the news half-way through my recovery I realised why my parents hadn't been in touch with me. They were concerned that it might cause me a serious setback, one that I might not recover from. They thought quite rightly that it might send me over the edge.

As it happened, however, I was about to move in the opposite direction.

* * *

I had been at Cottonwood for ten days when I suddenly understood what I was there for. I'd finally got it. I woke up in the middle of the night at about four or five in the morning. I was hot and I couldn't breathe. I got out of bed and went outside on to the veranda and lit a cigarette. It's quite a spiritual place, Arizona, and one of my favourite things to do there was to sit in the dark and watch what they call the Phoenix Lights. As I sat there listening to the sound of the coyotes, looking at the stars and watching the colour of the sky change from deep black to golden blue, for the first time in years I became very aware of my physical surroundings. It was like nothing that I had ever seen before. For the past ten years I hadn't opened my eyes. It was as though I had been blind for all that time. And I had certainly never seen a dawn like this. If I'd been up at that hour two months before it would have been because I was doing drugs. And if dawn was coming up then it would have been over some housing estate in Bermondsey.

All of a sudden here I am in the middle of something really beautiful, I thought to myself, It was spectacular. I wanted to see this again, and I wanted Kevin to see this with me.

I suddenly felt very aware of myself, my own physical being, my breathing. 'You're here, you're alive,' an inner voice said to me. 'It's a miracle.

You were put on this earth to be a lot more than a drug addict. You don't want to die a drug addict. You can do this – you can. You can survive this.'

I felt very small sitting there looking into the desert. I felt very humble. Who was I in the greater scheme of things? I was nothing. I was no one. I was just a tiny little dot on this mammoth map. I was here now, but if I carried on like this, I would be gone tomorrow. Being famous wasn't important, all that mattered was that you were there for those people who cared for you. All that I could be in this world was close to the people who would still have me: my parents, my brothers, Kevin maybe, and my children – my son Kai and this little baby who lay inside me.

First thing the next day I spoke to my psychiatrist and told her about my spiritual awakening. I asked whether it would be possible for me to call Kevin later that day and she agreed.

'It's me!' I said when he picked up the phone.

'Danni?'

'Yes it's me,' I said, laughing and smiling. My voice was full of happiness. I don't think Kevin had ever heard me like that in his life before.

'I've got it, I've cracked it. I'm going to get well and I'm going to come home. I want this more than anything. I want to live and be well. I want it for you, for Kai, for our baby and I want it for me!'

He was speechless.

The next few weeks of my recovery went like a

breeze. I enjoyed every moment I had at Cottonwood and took as much from the course that I could. I went to every lecture and meeting there was and read every book I could lay my hands on. I went to the desert on my trails, and I screamed and shouted in the wilderness. I happily skipped through my twelve steps to recovery. I slept well and I ate for Britain, for Tucson, Arizona and for my baby. For the first time in my life I felt free and alive. I could breathe at last and it felt great.

It was common practice at the clinic to swap meds. Everyone was at it and to start with, being the rebel I was, I was quite into the idea. You could take someone's upper when they wanted your downer and that way get the kick you craved for. But now that I had decided that I was going to make a go of things I decided that wasn't for me. I didn't want to play around any more.

I even managed to make friends there. There was a woman from Pennsylvania I used to spend time with who was a sex addict. She looked perfectly ordinary on the outside. She was married, to a plastic surgeon no less, and was the mother of three young girls. She was really normal except for the fact that she was addicted to sex. It didn't matter who she had it with – men, women, she didn't care so long as she had it. Needless to say I was riveted by her stories. Then there was a sixteen-year-old girl who was hooked on drugs and alcohol. She was so bad that once an armed SWAT team raided her house in the middle of the night to arrest her. And there was my other friend, a native American Indian woman in her sixties, who was addicted to prescription drugs. I met all sorts of people there from so many different walks of life. And the best thing about being there was that nobody knew me. Unlike the times I had gone to the Priory and had to sit in a room doing group sessions with a whole load of people you knew just couldn't wait to get home and blab that they had been in rehab with Danniella Westbrook, these people didn't care. They had no idea who I was, they had never seen *EastEnders* and that made me realise just how small I really was. For years I thought I was someone, but what I realised there was that I wasn't. Fame suddenly meant nothing to me; that world I had moved in, that life I had led – it was all so spurious.

I was just coming round to this way of thinking when, on my third week in rehab, I was sitting on my veranda and a helicopter started circling the building. It was making a hell of a racket and seemed to be just hovering overhead. Suddenly a voice came over the clinic's tannoy: 'Danniella, get back in the clinic, if you are outside please move back into the building.'

It turned out that a freelance photographer working for a British tabloid had chartered the helicopter from the local airfield on the off chance that he could get a picture of me in recovery. I simply couldn't believe it. It was such an invasion of my privacy. Sure, take a picture of me when I am off my head, print a picture of my damaged nose, put me on the front cover of your paper when I'm falling out of a club, by all means. Show me checking into rehab if that helps tell a story about the dangers of drug abuse. I deserve that, and if it stops people from taking drugs then that's brilliant too. But when I am in that clinic, trying to get well, when I am doing the best I can to sort my life out, when I am actually beginning to get better, please leave me alone. This is my time.

I was so annoyed about it. It just seemed like such a pointless thing to do. What did the photographer expect to see? Me walking round the complex in a strait-jacket accompanied by two armed guards? Had he got the photograph of me he would have been very disappointed. He would have captured a happy, healthy-looking girl sitting in a chair on a veranda reading the Narcotics Anonymous handbook as she stroked her pregnant tummy.

After five weeks at Cottonwood I was ready to go home. I didn't feel ready, I didn't want to leave, but that's what the doctors ordered. I had grown to like it there and I felt very happy and secure in that environment. Now I was going to have to take a giant step and go back to living in the real world, on my own. There was no Luc to help me this time. He had returned to the UK after he had put me here. I was alone and I was incredibly scared. Would I make it? Would I survive out there? At Cottonwood it was easy to stay clean, as there were no temptations there, but what would I feel like when I was back at home? Would I go out and score drugs the moment my feet hit the ground in London, as I had after I returned from Barbados?

I was driven to the airport and boarded a flight from Phoenix to LA. So far so good. I could deal with that part of the journey. But when I got to LA I discovered that my flight to London was delayed by two hours. That meant I had a four-hour wait at the airport on my own. I panicked at the prospect of it. I went to the loo, locked myself in a cubicle and sat on the floor and just cried and cried, rocking back and forth.

'Help, help me someone, please.'

I took a deep breath and I started to say the serenity prayer they had taught me at Cottonwood over and over again. I was like a rabbit caught in the headlights.

I didn't feel any better. I came out of the loo and rang my psychiatrist at Cottonwood and asked her if I could come back.

'No, Danni, you can't come back,' she said, almost laughing at me. 'You'll get through it, you will.'

I rang Kevin, still crying.

'Come on, baby,' he said. 'You'll be fine. You're strong now. You can do it.'

I could do it. I would do it.

I wiped my eyes and walked over to the bar and sat down. A waiter came over.

'Can I get you something to drink, Ma'am?'

'Yes, please, that would be nice.'

'What can I get you?'

'I'd like a Diet Coke, please.'

And so I sat there for the next four hours, drinking coke, eating a sandwich and reading a magazine. And, you know, it wasn't that bad after all.

The journey back to London was problem free and it couldn't have been more different to the one I had taken to LA. I genuinely felt like a new person, and in a way I was happy to go back because I was on a mission to sort my life out once and for all.

After Cottonwood it had been suggested that I go into secondary treatment as an outpatient at a centre in Florida for three months. I was keen on the idea, because I thought it was a good way of adjusting back to normal life slowly. But rather than go straight there, which would have been the most practical thing to do given that I was already in the States, I had to return to London for four days to go to court to fight for the custody of my son.

I had just one day to get re-acquainted with Kevin, who was overjoyed at my recovery. And it was good to be home with him too. But now I had to concentrate all my efforts on the court case and getting my son back where he belonged.

I was shaking when I arrived at the High Court in London.

'I can't lose Kai,' I said to Kevin. 'I just can't, it

would kill me.' He took me by the arm and told me not to worry.

The judge said that, provided a number of conditions were fulfilled by me, in eight months' time he would grant me custody of Kai. I was so happy and grateful I could not stop crying. Now I could get on with the next stage of my recovery.

Returning to the States was strange for me. This time I was completely on my own. There was no Luc to hold my hand on the plane, and I felt quite lonely and sad. Going back to London had made me realise how much I missed Kai and my home life. But I knew that I had to do this. Many people who go into rehab make the mistake of thinking that after a five-week boot camp in Arizona they will be cured from their addiction for good, but it doesn't really work like that. There is no miracle cure for addiction, it is a daily, ongoing battle. I hadn't been cured of my coke addiction at Cottonwood, but my stay there had taught me that it was possible to live without drugs, that I could have another life. What I had to do now was to put the lessons I learnt at Cottonwood into practice. My three-month stint as an outpatient in Florida was going to help me re-adjust the real world.

I was glad I was an outpatient, because the treatment centre itself wasn't a nice place. While I was there twelve in-patients relapsed on crack, so I think it was good for me to be away from that world at night. Also it was very important for me to learn to stand on my own two feet and to deal with being alone and having time on my hands.

I rented a small apartment near to the centre and quickly formed a routine. Each morning after I'd made myself breakfast I'd get ready and then drive to the centre, where I would attend a meeting until lunchtime. During my break I would go for a walk, and after I had eaten something I'd go to another meeting. When that was over I'd shop for my supper, return to the flat and sit there for the rest of the evening reading or watching films. It was a very simple life but one that I needed. I was calm, I was rested and I was learning to be on my own. It wasn't easy to start with, and there were times when all I wanted was either to return to Cottonwood or fly back to London to be with Kevin and my family. But I knew that I had to do this, because until I learnt to live on the outside on my own, without anyone else, and without any drugs, I hadn't really recovered.

17
THE HAPPY ENDING

....

They call the first year of your life as a recovering addict your honeymoon period. You are so excited to be clean and well, so pleased that you have managed to create a new life for yourself, that the picture just couldn't seem any rosier. When I returned from Florida in July 2001 I couldn't stop smiling. I was just so happy, it felt like walking on air. I was back together with Kevin, I had Kai's homecoming to look forward to and a baby on the way. I had never felt better.

I didn't want drugs, let alone crave them, in fact nothing could have been further from my mind. All I wanted was to be clean and to stay that way. I didn't need drugs any more – I was high on the life that I had. I was happy and content and looking forward to the future.

Kevin couldn't believe the change in me. He had never seen me this way, it was as though he was with a completely new person, as if all the psychosis, the madness, the aggression and the selfishness had been drawn out of me. I had a permanent grin on my face, took pleasure from the simplest things and was loving and affectionate. All I wanted was to be with him and be happy. Physically I had changed too. When I went to Arizona I had been three months pregnant, but I was so thin that you wouldn't have known it to look at me. Now as I moved into my third trimester I was blooming. I was as big as a house and I didn't care. I loved getting bigger and bigger by the day. I loved eating and I loved my food. I felt so healthy and so very pregnant. When Kai was on the way I was too out of it and too ill to derive any pleasure or feeling from having a child grow within me, but this time round it was different. There were other physical changes in me too. My skin was clear and radiant. The dark circles had gone from under my eyes, there was colour in my cheeks, and my hair and my nails had begun to grow again. My face was rounder and less gaunt, and my legs and arms had some shape to them. It was as though I was a new person both inside and out.

I spent the next couple of months nesting at home, preparing for the birth and for Kai to come back to me. I was so excited. I felt like a child waiting for Christmas. Kevin started working from home and so we spent all our time with each other, building our new life together, making plans for the future.

Our daughter Jodie was born on Wednesday 5 September 2001 at the Portland Hospital. I had planned to have a natural birth but she finished up in the breech position, so in the end I had to have an emergency caesarean. I didn't mind, I was just glad that she was alive. Although the doctors had told me she would be fine, it still preyed on my mind that there might be something wrong with her given that I was three months pregnant when I overdosed. I had nothing to worry about. Like Kai she too had almost miraculously not been affected by my drug abuse, and when she was delivered she came out crying like a little fighter, weighing in at a very respectable 6lb 14oz.

I had always assumed that Kevin wanted me to have a boy, as he already had a daughter from his first marriage. I suspected too that he wanted a son and heir to pass his business on to, but when I asked him whether he was disappointed he just laughed.

'You are joking,' he said as he cradled her in his arms for the first time. 'Look at her, she's beautiful. She looks just like you. Anyway I've got Kai, he's my heir. I'm grooming him to take over my empire when I retire!'

Two months later Kai came home and our family unit was complete. I was over the moon to see him again, my little boy. It felt so good to be with him and to be clean. I can't describe what it felt like to tuck him into bed at night and read him his story, to be there for him in the morning when he woke, to do all the simple things that a parent should. I'd take him to the park to feed the ducks with Jodie in her pram. We'd go

shopping, play football, watch children's films together. It felt good to be with Kai without being high,
drunk or hung over. It felt good just to be normal.

I thought for a while that my life couldn't get better
than this, but I was wrong, for on 27 December that
year Kevin and I got married. It was a huge wedding
and we made sure that all the people who mattered to
us were there. Kevin's family didn't come, but he had
mine and they already loved him as if he was their own
son anyway.

When my mother came into my room before the
service and saw me in my white, floor-length, strapless
wedding dress, my hair put up in a chignon, with a
diamond tiara pinning it into place, and holding my
bouquet of red roses, she burst into tears. I suppose it's
normal for a mother to get emotional on their daughter's wedding day, but this was taking it a bit far. She
was sobbing!

'What's wrong, Mum? What is it? Is it the dress? Is
it the hair? Aren't you happy for me?'

She came over and hugged me.

'Of course I'm happy for you, darling,' she said. 'It's
just I never thought I would see this day. I always
thought I'd be going to your funeral, not your wedding.'

After the service we sat down for dinner and I
looked round the room and smiled. Here were all
the people I really loved, my parents, my brothers, my
children, my friends, Michael Grecco and Barbara

Windsor, Denise Van Outen, my *EastEnders* co-star Dean Gaffney, Luc and Angela. And I looked at my husband, this wonderful man who had given me a second chance at life.

'I'm so happy to be your wife,' I said. 'I'm so happy not to be Danniella Westbrook any more, but Danniella Jenkins, Mrs Kevin Jenkins!' And with that we toasted each other's health and happiness with a glass of Red Bull.

I am sometimes asked, by people who are either suffering from cocaine addiction themselves or know someone who is, whether I think that Cottonwood is the best place to go if you want to make a full recovery. My answer to that is always no. Whilst I would always recommend it on the strength of what it did for me, I think what people have to understand about recovery is that it isn't so much a question of where you go but *when* you go. When you go into treatment it has to be because *you* really want to recover. It can't just be because your family or your friends want you to go down that route. If it is going to work then you have to make the decision that *you* are going to make it work.

One of the reasons why I relapsed when I came out of treatment in the past was because I had never put my heart in to it. There is no point in sitting in a clinic for five weeks abstaining from everything if all you are thinking about when you are in there is when and where you will get your next fix. There is no point in getting clean if you are not going to make any effort to stay clean. When I first went to the Priory all I did all day was think about when I was going to take drugs again. When I first went to the Nightingale and ran away in the night I did so purely because I wanted to take cocaine. During a second time in there I'm ashamed to admit I even ended up taking crack with another addict in his room. I had actually never used the drug before but I was desperate for a hit of some kind while I was in there, so I smoked it with him, I was that bad. It was a very dangerous thing to do because I really liked it and I ended up doing it again a couple of times in shady crack houses. But even I had the sense to stop. I knew that if I carried on taking it I would be dead within weeks. Why Cottonwood worked for me that time was that I realised that I didn't want to die, I didn't want to end up as just another statistic on the books. I didn't want my son to have to grow up telling his friends that his mother had died from an overdose. Why Cottonwood worked for me was that for the first time in my life *I* wanted to be clean.

For this reason it annoys me when I see stories in the press about celebrities and their drug and drink problems. What usually happens once one of the tabloids has run their exposé is that these people are within days forced into rehab to supposedly sort themselves out, to dry out, clean up and get their lives back on track. And it is only when they have booked themselves into a clinic that they are left alone. Only then are we allowed to sympathise with them. Until then they are just shameless drug addicts or alcoholics. But in my experience that doesn't actually help anyone. Yes, it *might* give you the wake-up call you need. Yes, it *might* shame you into changing your way of life. But the only way you are ever going to recover from your addiction is if you decide that you no longer want to live your life like that. It's not up to the press, it's not even up to your family or your friends. At the end of the day it's up to you.

There is no miracle cure for addiction, either. Recovery doesn't end when you check out of a clinic, or a hospital or an outpatient treatment centre. Recovery is an ongoing process. You have to carry on fighting that battle every day for the rest of your life. When I returned home from Florida I was well and happy, and pleased that I was clean, but I knew that if I wanted to stay that way I was going to have to work at it. And I did.

For two years I went to meetings. I started with Cocaine Anonymous, then went to Narcotics Anonymous and then Alcoholics Anonymous. Sometimes I would go to all three in one week. I went to conventions, I read as much literature as I could, I made friends with people who were in the same boat as me. Why did I do all this? Because I didn't want to go back to being the person I was before, it was as simple as that. And I discovered that by going to these meetings and surrounding myself with people who had similar problems to myself I could get through this. You see, you can sit with a counsellor and talk about yourself and your problems until you are blue in the face, but unless they have been to the place you have, unless they have sunk that low, unless they have had to fight the fight you have had to, then they can't really understand who you are. They may very well have lots of initials after their name, but only an addict knows what it is really like to walk in your shoes, has sat where you are sitting. Only they understand the constant, daily fight one has to engage in to stay clean.

I admit that I was very lucky in that I was able to afford to go to Cottonwood. At over £3,000 a week that kind of treatment does not come cheap, but what I would say to anyone who can't afford to go that route is that there are other ways. As long as you are ready to put your heart into it, attending a meeting with recovering addicts in your local coffee shop can be just as helpful as sitting in a clinic in the middle of the desert in Arizona. What recovery is all about is seeing the light, seeing that you can live a life without drugs and that you can be happy. It's about being informed, about making a decision to change, about knowing that you have the strength within you to do so and having the support you need to take you through that process.

Anyone I came into contact with during those first few months out of recovery couldn't believe the change in me. I was together, content and well adjusted. I had turned the corner, there was no question about that, and had successfully managed to put my past behind me. I was living in a lovely house with my husband and my two children, going on the school run, shopping at the supermarket, taking my kids to the park. On the face of it I was just an ordinary housewife, living an ordinary but very happy life.

I was clean, I was happy, and I was healthy. I felt good, that was for sure, but I knew that if I was really going to feel like a new person, if I was really going to put my past behind me and start again, then I was going to have to do something about my nose. I was going to have to see whether someone could put my face back together.

For so many years I had lived without a nose and it hadn't really bothered me. As disturbing as this sounds, so long as I could get cocaine up it I hadn't really cared what I looked like, not even with Kevin. The poor man had never even known me with a nose, so it hadn't really been an issue. But now that I was clean it really began to bother me. I would look in the mirror when I went to put my make-up on or brush my hair or teeth, and feel sickened by what I saw before me. I looked like a monster. Now that I was clean I could see for the first time how others saw me. I had been too out of it before to care, but now I had all my wits about me I really began to mind about it. How could I have done this to myself? How could I have deformed myself in this way? And for the first time in my life I thought about how it must affect other people to see me like this. My mother and father, my poor brothers, all the people I had worked with. And I thought about what it must be like for Kevin. As I looked in the mirror, at this gaping hole in my face, where my septum should have been, I saw what he saw during our most intimate moments together. Kevin, bless him, always said it didn't bother him, but there was another person in my life for whom I knew it was a real problem, and that was Kai.

Not long after he came home to me, Kai and I were talking in the kitchen one day and I was trying to explain to him why he had been sent away to live with his father.

'Do you remember when I was ill, Kai?'

'Yes, I do Mummy.'

'And you know I went away to get better?'

'Yes,'

'Well, that's why you had to go and stay with your Daddy.'

'And are you well now, Mummy?'

'Yes, I'm much better, Kai. They mended me and made me well again for you.'

And he looked up at me and said: 'Will they mend your nose too, Mummy?'

It was difficult for Kai because he had just started going to school. I may have learnt to conceal my nose from other people, but it's quite another thing when you are standing in a school cloakroom trying to put your son's coat on at the end of the day and you have ten little children staring up at you. Believe me, there is no hiding it then. And I know they used to say things to him. And I know it upset him. When I used to ask him what he wanted for his birthday or Christmas the answer was always the same: 'A nose for Mummy.'

One day we were out together with my mother at the Bluewater shopping centre, in Kent, when a woman came up to me.

'It's you, isn't it?' she said. 'That girl from *East-Enders*.'

'Er, yes, yes it's me,' I said, somewhat embarrassed.

For one foolishly vain moment I thought she was going to ask for my autograph, but instead she grabbed her children, who can't have been more than eleven or twelve, and pushed them under my face.

'Ere, you lot, take a good look at 'er face. That's what you'll end up looking like if you do drugs.'

I almost wanted to laugh at the situation it was so comic, and had it not been for Kai I would have done, but he was very upset. He still didn't know what drugs were, but he knew this woman was having a go at me because of my nose.

I vowed after that to get it seen to. There was no point in being a normal mum to Kai if I didn't look like one.

It took me a while to summon up the courage to call Mr Frame. I was so ashamed by what I had done to my nose following that first operation that I didn't think I could face him again. However, I had consulted nearly every plastic surgeon on Harley Street and none of them seemed able to help me. Eventually I swallowed my pride, picked up the phone and called him.

'Mr Frame? It's Danniella here, Danniella Westbrook. Remember me?' I ventured nervously.

'Danniella! Good to hear from you,' he said cheerfully. 'I wondered when I was going to hear from you! When are you coming to see me?'

It took a lot of collagen, a piece of shark's cartilage, two operations and one very skilled surgeon to get my nose back to normal again. It wasn't a straightforward process and I was very lucky to have Mr Frame, because otherwise I don't think it would have worked. But he had done a great deal of research into how he was going to rebuild it and gave me options as to how it could be done. My main concern was that I didn't look too weird after the surgery, because I didn't want to upset the children. But he managed to reconstruct it in such an unobtrusive way that I only had a small bandage and dressing on my face after each procedure. He even found me an anaesthetist who was experienced with working with drug addicts. One of their main concerns was not to use any drug during or after the operation that was remotely addictive in any way. After nine months and two surgeries my nose was back to normal, and last year I went through a final procedure, where collagen was injected into my septum to give it some definition. Finally I was back to normal; finally I could, quite literally, hold my head up high again.

Eighteen months after I returned from Florida, I began to discover why they call your first year of being clean your honeymoon period. For the first year I had been so happy to be alive and well that I was in a constant state of euphoria. I was busy adjusting to my new way of life, spending time with the baby and looking after Kai. Kevin had stayed at home for most of that first year, so I always had him to lean on, to talk to.

But after a while things changed. Our own honeymoon was over. We were still very much in love, of course, but we came down off our wedding high and got back to living real life. Jodie had got into her routine, Kai was at school most of the day, and Kevin returned to work because he was having a few problems at the office. And so I suddenly found myself home alone without that much to do. There is only so much housework or cooking a girl can do, and once Jodie was down for her nap I'd find myself in the kitchen staring at the walls wondering what to do next. Maybe I should go shopping? Maybe I should make myself some lunch? Maybe I'd have a bath?

And it was during these moments that I found my recovery very hard. I would think, is this it? Is this all there is? And I would get very down. I know it sounds irrational. I had the life most people dream of, but the fact was I was bored. When you are an addict you are constantly searching for stimulation in your life; when you are in recovery you have to learn to live without it. For a while I managed to get by, and when I felt like this I'd ring Beechy. Sometimes we would talk about my addiction, sometimes we would just talk about trivial things like what I had been doing that day. If I was very blue I would take myself off to a meeting and after that I would feel better for a while.

It's not that I wanted to take drugs. I didn't. My life just felt a bit empty and I wasn't sure what to do with it. I had too much time on my hands. And so I decided that maybe I should return to work. I had been working since the age of seven, after all, and it was what I knew. It was what I liked doing. I didn't think I could survive as a housewife for the rest of my life.

After making a few tentative calls to see what was on offer I was approached by the producers of the reality show *I'm a Celebrity, Get Me Out of Here!* to appear in the programme. It was May 2003. I was in two minds about doing it. I wasn't sure I was ready to leave Kevin and the kids behind and spend two weeks in the Australian jungle without them. Kevin wasn't too thrilled by the idea either but he said that he would respect my decision if that's what I wanted to do. The producers on the other hand were very keen. They told me how it would be a great opportunity for me to turn my life around, that by appearing on the show I could let the public see what I was really like for the first time. If I did this, they argued, people would see me for who I was, not just as a former soap star with addiction problems or the 'girl with no nose'. That sold it to me.

And so I flew to Australia and entered the jungle. Amongst the other celebrities there were the chef Antony Worrall Thompson, the cricketer Phil Tufnell, Wayne Sleep, John Fashanu and Sian Lloyd, the weather girl. We were allowed one luxury item to take in with us. I chose the AA handbook. I wasn't scared about roughing it in the jungle. Despite my penchant for designer clothes, manicures and make-up I am quite tough at heart. I had been going to the gym regularly since I got clean, so I was fit, and I had survived Cottonwood. How bad could this be? But what I hadn't bargained for was the distress I would feel at leaving my husband and my babies behind. This was the first time I was going to be separated from them since we got Kai back, and from the moment I left the house and waved them goodbye I had a sinking feeling in my heart.

Once I entered the jungle itself things didn't get any better. Right from the word go I knew I wanted to 'get out of there' as they say on the show. It had nothing to do with the conditions, the tasks, the lack of food, the bugs or the other contestants either for that matter. It had to do with me. I thought I was strong enough to do this, but I wasn't. I need to be around my family and my friends. I wasn't ready for this. When you are a recovering addict you need to feel that you always have a support system there for you if you crack. Even if you don't actually need it, you need to know it's there for you in the background, a phone call away. All I had round me were cameras, and believe me that isn't a good thing when you are going through what I was.

I was so unhappy those first few days that I went to talk to the producers via the 'Bush Telegraph' and told them I didn't think I was up to it, but they didn't want me to leave. They begged me to stay, they even got a shrink in there to persuade me not to walk, which, looking back, given her qualifications, was highly irresponsible of her. And so they talked me round and I stayed in the jungle, but all that happened was that I got more and more upset and would cry and cry. And all they did about this was film me, because I guess it made great TV. By day nine I'd had enough. I had to go. I needed to see Kevin. It was the longest time I had been away from him since I had been in America and I couldn't cope. I couldn't cope without the children and without knowing I could talk to a counsellor if I needed to.

The night before I walked I lay in my hammock and thought it through. I didn't need to do this. I had already achieved what I needed to by getting clean. What was I trying to prove to myself? What lesson was I really learning here? All it had taught me was that I was unable to cope in this environment. This wasn't even the real world, it was a fake one. And if I had to put my hand up and admit that I could not survive as a recovering drug addict without a network of support from people who knew, loved or understood me, then so be it. I was only human.

Most celebrities go on shows like that to raise their profiles, which is great. But what I realised whilst I was there was that I no longer cared about my profile. I no longer cared about being famous, or living on planet celebrity. I didn't need to do that. I was lucky enough to have everything I wanted, and it was right there back at home waiting for me.

So the following morning I packed my bag, said goodbye to the others, and having got the support of all of them, I walked over the bridge and said goodbye to that world for ever. I no longer wanted to be famous for the sake of it. I no longer wanted to be a celebrity. I wanted to be a wife and a mother. I wanted to be clean and free and alive and well. And most of all I wanted to be myself.

When I'd made the decision to walk off *I'm a Celebrity* . . . and come out of the jungle I can't begin to describe just how free I felt. I wasn't worried what people thought of me, I just didn't care. They could think anything they wanted about me – that I was a coward, that I was spoilt, that I was a two-bit former junkie – it meant nothing to me. For the first time in my life it no longer mattered. And that was the most liberating feeling of all. From the moment I started performing at the age of seven all I cared about was what people thought of me. But I could see now just how ridiculous that is, because all it ever was was a performance. When I was modelling in a commercial as a child, when I played Sam in *EastEnders*, when I was Dawn in *Frank Stubbs Presents*, when I was standing in a sexy bra and knickers on the cover of some lads' magazine, all of that was just an act. It wasn't me. People were entitled to their opinion of me, whichever way it went. When you stand up on stage and shout 'look at me' then you have to be prepared to take the bad with the good.

The producers of *I'm a Celebrity* . . . had told me that by going on the show I would give people the chance to see the 'real' me, but did that really matter? In any case when you are being filmed round the clock twenty-four seven don't think for a moment that anyone, especially those who are paid to be in the public eye, ever dares show their real self. The real me is not the girl on the telly trying to be all sweetness and light on a reality show in order to win a prize. The real me is the woman driving up the back of you on the motorway because she is running late for a meeting. The real me is the mother who's feeling a little bit frayed in the morning because she has been up all night with a child with a fever. The real me is the wife who's getting a little bit lippy with her husband because he doesn't understand why she is feeling frayed that day. She is the woman who doesn't look so great without her make-up on, who could do with her highlights being retouched and when she looks in the mirror thinks about Botox. That is the real me.

Once out of the jungle I was driven to the Versace Hotel, on the Gold Coast, where all the contestants and their families were being put up after they came out of the show, and was reunited with Kevin. I couldn't believe how happy I was to see him. It felt like I had come home. I flung my arms round him and said to him, 'Never, ever, let me do anything like that again.'

He laughed. 'It's good to have you back.'

'It's good to be back,' I said.

After nine days in the jungle, living on the most meagre of rations, I should have been excited about the prospect of food and I was told that I could pick from any of the delicacies off the hotel menu and charge it to the show, but all I wanted was a Big Mac.

'I'm not very showbiz any more, am I?' I said to Kevin as I took a hungry bite from my burger.

'No, thankfully you're not,' he said smiling.

Kevin and I sat in our room that night talking and came to some decisions about our future together. I knew as well as he did that I couldn't just sit at home all day and do nothing, as nice as the idea was. I had to work, it was all I had ever known. I enjoyed it and I liked making my own money, but I promised him and myself that I wouldn't do anything that took me away from him or my children again.

My attitude to fame and the notion of celebrity had

changed. It was no longer important to me. It was no longer a priority. I still wanted to work but the fact was, and still is today, that I didn't know any world other than that. I'd never had another job, other than my brief stint serving drinks in the social club. I didn't have another skill, and I didn't really have any qualifications.

'What do you think I should do?' I asked Kevin as we lay in bed that night.

'Do what you want to do. Follow your heart,' he said. 'Carry on in this world if that works for you, just don't take it too seriously and never let it come between us.' He yawned, rolled over and fell asleep.

The reaction from the press and the public to my exit from the show was a lot more favourable than I thought it would be. In fact I had been given a huge amount of support, which was touching. Kevin and I spent the next few days holed up in our hotel room fielding requests for interviews. They were all offering silly amounts of money.

'What should I do?' I asked him.

'Do it,' he said in his straightforward way. 'Do it, charge them and then give all the money to charity. That's what you should do.' And that's exactly what I did.

18
ONE DAY AT A TIME

....

My name is Danniella, and I am an addict.

These are the words I stand up and say every time I attend a meeting of Alcoholics or Narcotics Anonymous. It is a small sentence, just nine words long, but it is one that took me many years to finally be able to say. It is a simple but defining statement about who I am. I am an addict, and I will be till the day I die.

When I look back to how I was then sometimes it feels like I am watching a film, or reading a book about someone else. There are times when I can't believe that this really is my life story. I cannot believe that I really was that person. My life today is so different from what it was back then, it is as though I don't know that girl any more, as though she is a stranger to me. That whole world is now so alien to me that I cannot believe that I ever belonged to it. When I have these thoughts I know that I am having a good day.

And then there are moments in my life when it all

comes crashing down on me and I realise the pain and the hurt I caused through my addiction. I think of how I behaved, what I did. I think of the destruction I caused to those who loved me. I remember how I was with my parents and my brothers. I realise how much of their lives I took away from them. I look at my husband and wonder why he ever stood by me. I look at my children and cannot believe that they are even here with me now. I am lucky. In many ways I believe that I must be blessed, although I am not sure why. I don't know who or what was responsible for giving me a second chance in this life, all I know is that I didn't really deserve it. And with those thoughts comes this terrible, overwhelming sense of guilt and shame. I wonder at times how any of the people I loved yet hurt so much can still look me in the eye, because sometimes when I am standing in front of the mirror I find it quite difficult myself. When I have those thoughts I know that I am having a bad day.

But this is just part and parcel of my recovery. I may feel good about my future now, but I will never be that comfortable about my past.

When I returned to England from Australia, offers of work flooded in, but I took my time deciding what I wanted to do. I knew for the time being I didn't want to act. I had spent too long being other people and I was quite enjoying being myself for once. I turned down the modelling work because I didn't want to be seen in that way any more. I was approaching thirty, I was a wife and a mother, and somehow it didn't seem appropriate to be photographed half-naked across a magazine spread. I would keep that kind of look for my husband and spare Kai and Jodie the embarrassment of having to see their mother like that.

I decided that for now if I did any work then I would like to present television programmes and that would be it for the time being. The deal I struck with Kevin was that the programmes had to be based in the UK and they couldn't take me away from him and the kids for more than five days at a time. I also decided that I would only work on programmes that interested me, the ones I might watch if I was in at home. What was important to me was that I wouldn't take work on just for the sake of being on TV. I couldn't do it for fame, I had to do it for other reasons. And so the first job I took on was a live television series about plastic surgery. Obviously it was a subject close to my heart. Having had my nose rebuilt and undergone breast enhancement surgery to make me feel a little more confident about my physical appearance following my recovery, I knew what a difference these procedures could make to a person's life. The next programme I worked on was a series about hauntings and ghosts, shown on satellite television. Again, I took the job because it interested me. I have always been fascinated by anything to do with the supernatural. So, to date, this has been my approach to work. I can't just do something for fame or money, because I no longer need those things in my life. It has to be for the love of the job.

More than anything else, these days I am motivated by the need to make people understand addiction and the danger of drugs. I decided a long time ago now that if I was going to use my notoriety in any way then it would be to tell the story of my addiction, because if that can persuade just one impressionable young person not to take drugs or help one addict with problems as severe as mine realise that there is a way out, then that's a good thing. I don't mind being a poster girl for drugs awareness any more, it's a lot more worthwhile than being one for a bar of soap or a supermarket chain. As far as I am concerned they can put up posters of me and my damaged nose all round the country for everyone to see. So long as people get the message that this is what drugs can do to you, then that's absolutely fine by me.

The other day I went back to the Sylvia Young school to meet with some of the pupils there, and as I made my way to the classroom I noticed a poster for a drugs awareness helpline and I was really pleased about that. We didn't have that in my day. I can't say for sure that, if we had, I wouldn't have tried drugs when I was fourteen, but at least I would have had someone to talk to about it afterwards. It's a start anyway.

*   *   *

I live a very quiet and ordinary life these days. When I am not working I spend my time doing what other women in my position do. I do the school run, do the laundry, feed the dogs, collect the dry cleaning, get the car serviced and decide what we are going to have for dinner that night. At weekends I watch Kai play sport, take Jodie swimming and sit outside the video shop for what seems like hours as Kai and Jordan squabble about what DVD they want that night. When Kevin comes back from work we chat about our day, flick the telly on and lie on the sofa talking through our list of things to do in the house. I can't say our marriage is perfect – whose is? We fight, we argue, we annoy each other from time to time, but we also really love each other and I think the fact that we have survived through so much together is testimony to that.

Kevin and I don't drink any more, but neither of us minds about it or misses it. In the way that other couples might get stuck into a nice bottle of wine in the evening we crack into the Diet Coke and have found other ways to unwind. We rarely go out to any celebrity functions, as that just doesn't interest Kevin, and on the rare occasions when we do it will be because it is a charity event or something that we can take the children to. These days our social life revolves around our children and our family and friends. It may sound tedious to some, but I can honestly say I have never been happier.

Sure, I have bad days and suffer from depression at

times, which is difficult because there isn't much medication you can take for that when you are a recovering drug addict. But I pull myself out of those moods. I ring Beechy and talk to him for hours, which helps me. As a recovering alcoholic himself he can relate to my good days and my bad ones too. When I have time I go to a meeting, but I don't go every day. Frankly, I don't have the time to spend all day talking about my problems in a coffee shop, as much as I would like to. I also believe that there is a point in recovery when you have to move on. It's all about crossing the bridge to the other side, to a normal life. I don't want to become addicted to being an addict. I don't want to live my life in the past – it's time for me to move on.

Sometimes that's easier said than done. I am conscious of what people think of me, aware that there are those who still think of me as the girl with no nose, as a coke addict. Sometimes, when I am out to dinner with my husband and between courses I get up to go to the bathroom, I am only too aware of what other people are thinking. 'There she goes, Danniella Westbrook, off to take another line of coke.'

There was a time, five years ago, when they would have been right and wholly justified in thinking that, but not any more. I am a different person today.

My name is Danniella, and I am a cocaine addict. But I am a lot of other things too. I am a wife, a mother, a daughter, a sister, an aunt and a friend, and when I die eventually that is how I would like to be remembered. As someone who went through a battle with addiction but survived it, to come back and reclaim her life. As someone who made it to the other side of nowhere.